omelettes
perfect anytime

pictured on cover
smoked salmon delight, page 24

Omelettes – Perfect Anytime
by the Canadian Egg Marketing Agency

First Printing – May 2003

Copyright© 2003
Canadian Egg Marketing Agency

Published by
Centax Books/Publishing Solutions
1150 Eighth Avenue, Regina, Saskatchewan, Canada S4R 1C9

Canadian Cataloguing in Publication Data

Main entry under title:

Omelettes : perfect anytime / Canadian Egg Marketing Agency.

Published also in French under title: Les omelettes: idéales à tout moment.
Includes index.
ISBN 1-894022-87-4

1. Omelettes. I. Canadian Egg Marketing Agency.
TX745.O43 2003   641.6'75   C2003-910705-1

Photography by Patricia Holdsworth
Patricia Holdsworth Photography
Regina, Saskatchewan

Cover and page design by Fantail Communications
Toronto, Ontario

Recipe testing by Pam Collacott
Home Economist, Trillium Cooking School
Ottawa, Ontario

Page formatting and index by Iona Glabus

Printed and Produced in Canada by Centax Books, a Division of PW Group
Publishing Director, Photo Designer & Food Stylist: Margo Embury
1150 Eighth Avenue, Regina, Saskatchewan, Canada S4R 1C9
(306) 525-2304   Fax: (306) 757-2439
centax@printwest.com   www.centaxbooks.com

table of contents

Welcome to a celebration of Canada's cooks! *Omelettes – Perfect Anytime* is a presentation of a sampling of the omelette recipes that best showcase the talents of family cooks across Canada.

In the summer of 2002, the Canadian Egg Marketing Agency urged Canadians to think outside of the box and use eggs in creative and heart-healthy ways. Omelettes as quick and healthy meal solutions was the message presented by Operation Omelette, a coast-to-coast tour that show-cased great ways to get creative with eggs. The tour also emphasized the fact that eggs meet the criteria for the Heart and Stroke Foundation's Health Check™ program.

The Operation Omelette team travelled across Canada, encountering many interesting situations and people, to present the notion that eggs are more than a great breakfast solution. In an attempt to capture the essence of Canada's culinary diversity, Canadians were encouraged to enter their favourite omelette recipes in a Recipe Rally contest.

Omelettes – Perfect Anytime is a compilation of the winning recipes from this national rally and presents the various tastes and talents of Canadians as more and more people adopt eggs as a quick meal solution.

Let's celebrate the cooks of Canada!

note

The recipes in this book have been tested in U.S. standard measurements. Common metric measurements are given as a convenience for those who are more familiar with metric. These recipes have not been tested in metric.

healthy eating –

More than ever, the egg is being recognized for its outstanding nutritional qualities. Nearly all the essential nutrients required for proper functioning of the human body are hiding inside that shell. Eggs are part of the Health Check™ program, an initiative of the Heart and Stroke Foundation of Canada to help you make wise and healthy food choices when grocery shopping. This is just one more sign that eggs are a healthy choice!

† Enjoying a variety of foods is part of healthy eating. Eggs are a nutritious food and should be eaten in moderation. Canadian egg producers financially support the Health Check™ education program. This is not an endorsement. See www.healthcheck.org

egg protein tops the chart

Did you know that egg protein is used as the standard for measuring other protein foods? That's because eggs provide some of the best-quality protein available. One large egg contains 6 grams of protein, only 70 calories and just 5 grams of fat. So enjoy… it's good to eat eggs!

high-density nutrition

Eggs are a unique food because they contain almost every nutrient known to be essential to humans. The egg white consists mainly of high-quality protein, and the yolk provides 11 essential vitamins and minerals, which both nourish the body and help maintain good health. Eggs are also an excellent source of choline, an essential nutrient that plays an important role in brain development and memory.[1] Eating eggs means eating better!

Nutrition Facts

Per 1 large egg (50 g)

Amount		% Daily Value
Calories 70		
Fat 5 g		8 %
Saturated 1.5 g + Trans 0 g		8 %
Cholesterol 190 mg		
Sodium 55 mg		2 %
Carbohydrate 0 g		0 %
Fibre 0 g		0 %
Sugars 0 g		
Protein 6 g		
Vitamin A	8 %	Vitamin C 0 %
Calcium	0 %	Iron 2 %
Vitamin D	2 %	Vitamin E 6 %
Riboflavin	15 %	Niacin 6 %
Vitamin B_{12}	30 %	Folate 15 %

Source: Health Canada, Canadian Nutrient File, 2001

[1] Hu et al. JAMA 1999; 281:1387-1394, N Engl J Med 1997; 337:1491-1499, BMJ 1996; 313:84-90, J Clin Epidemiol 1996; 49:211-216.

egg-cellent research

Recent research[1] has determined that eggs are one of nature's most nutritious foods and play an important role in maintaining a well-balanced diet. Indeed, eggs are highly nutritious and an excellent source of high-quality protein. They also provide significant amounts of several vitamins and minerals. Recent research[1] also indicates that egg eaters are more likely to have diets that provide proper amounts of essential nutrients.

eggs measure up as high-quality food

Canada's Food Guide to Healthy Eating considers 1 to 2 eggs to be a serving from the Meat and Alternatives group, proving that eggs are an important part of a well-balanced diet and a healthy lifestyle. Include eggs in your diet as they provide excellent nutritional value for just pennies!

keep an eye on eggs

Research[2] shows that lutein is important in maintaining healthy eyesight. Egg yolks contain lutein and zeaxanthin, two antioxidants from the carotenoid family that contribute to improving eye health and protecting eyes from ultraviolet rays. What's more, data from the Beaver Dam Eye Study[3] shows that people who eat eggs every day have less risk of developing cataracts.

take eggs to heart

One large egg contains just 5 grams of fat, of which only 1.5 grams is saturated. Best of all, it contains no *trans* fats. Whether you eat one egg a week or more than one egg a day, there's no evidence to support the notion that you increase your risk of cardiovascular disease, as long as you're in good health.[4] Go ahead and enjoy, you can probably eat more eggs than you think!

good news for the heart

It's time to give eggs a break! That's because, contrary to popular belief, eggs do not have a negative effect on blood cholesterol levels. In fact, a study by the prestigious Harvard School of Public Health found no significant link between eating eggs and developing cardiovascular disease in healthy individuals.[2] That's good news for people who love eggs!

1. The Role of Eggs in the Diet: Update – August 2002. A Special Report from the American Council on Science and Health.
2. Journal of the American College of Nutrition, Vol. 19, No. 5, 5225-5275 (2000).
3. Moeller et al. JACN 2000; (915s): 523s-527s.
4. Hu et al. JAMA 1999; 281:1387-1394, N Engl J Med 1997; 337:1491-1499, BMJ 1996; 313:84-90, J Clin Epidemiol 1996; 49:211-216.

handling eggs

buying eggs

- To ensure top quality, buy only Canada grade "A" eggs that have been kept refrigerated and that have clean, oval and uncracked shells.
- Check the "Best Before" date on the carton. It indicates the length of time the eggs will maintain their grade "A" quality. If you want to eat them after that date, they are best used in a thoroughly cooked dish.

storing eggs

- Eggs are perishable. When shopping, pick up eggs last. Get them home and into a refrigerator immediately.
- Store eggs in the refrigerator in their original carton. The carton prevents them from absorbing flavours and odours of other strong-smelling foods like onion, cheese or cabbage, and also serves as a reminder of the "Best Before" date.

cooking with eggs

All of the recipes in this book have been tested using large eggs. If you need to substitute eggs of other sizes for large eggs, use the chart below.

If a recipe calls for...	You can use...		
	Extra Large	Medium	Small
1 large egg	1	1	2
2 large eggs	2	2	3
3 large eggs	3	4	4
4 large eggs	3	5	6
5 large eggs	4	6	7
6 large eggs	5	7	8

Visit www.eggs.ca for more nutrition information, egg-handling tips and recipes!

basic omelette

As proven by the original recipes in this book, there are no limits to creative omelettes.

2 eggs	**2**
2 tbsp water*	**30 mL**
salt and pepper to taste	
1 tbsp butter OR **use cooking spray**	**15 mL**
filling of your choice	

A

1 Beat together eggs and water; season with salt and pepper (A).

2 Heat an 8" (20 cm) skillet over medium-high heat. Pour in egg mixture. As mixture sets at the edges, with spatula, gently push cooked portions toward the centre or lift edges to allow uncooked egg to flow underneath (B).

B

3 When egg is almost set on surface but still looks moist, cover half of the omelette with your choice of filling. Slip spatula under the unfilled side, fold the omelette in half and slide onto a warm plate (C).

C

Makes 1 serving
Preparation: 2 minutes
Cooking: 4 minutes

Nutrients per serving
Calories: 247   Protein: 12.4 g
Carbohydrate: 0.6 g   Fat: 21.4 g

* The use of water is preferred when making omelettes. The water turns to steam, producing a light, airy omelette.

tips
- Skillet is hot enough when a drop of water rolls around instead of bursting into steam.
- The proper skillet size is important. The right size skillet for a 1, 2 or 3-egg omelette is about 8" (20 cm) in diameter at the base. It should be shallow with sloping sides to make it easier to slide the omelette onto the plate.
- Always prepare individual omelettes rather than one large one. You will find them lighter, fluffier and easier to handle.
- Multiply the recipe for as many servings as you need. Use ½ cup (125 mL) of egg mixture for a 2-egg omelette and ¾ cup (175 mL) for a 3-egg omelette.

**black bean & salsa omelette,
page 26**

heart-healthy

apple frittata* with rosemary

The hint of rosemary adds an intriguing flavour to this very fruity omelette.

2 eggs, beaten	**2**
2 tsp water	**10 mL**
1 apple, peeled, finely diced	**1**
¼ tsp chopped fresh rosemary	**1 mL**
salt and pepper to taste	

Makes 1 serving
Preparation: 4 minutes
Cooking: 6 minutes

1 Combine all ingredients in a mixing bowl.

2 Spray a small non-stick skillet with cooking spray. Preheat to medium.

3 Pour egg mixture into skillet. As egg mixture sets at the edges, with spatula, gently lift cooked portion to allow uncooked egg to flow underneath. Cook until bottom is set and top is almost set.

4 Slide frittata onto a plate, then invert back into skillet. Cook another 1 to 2 minutes to cook second side.**

5 Serve on a warm plate.

Nutrients per serving
Calories: 218   Protein: 12.5 g
Carbohydrate: 19.7 g   Fat: 10.3 g

Bill Cole
Val Caron, Ontario

* Omelette vs. Frittata – the classic French omelette is traditionally folded over savory or sweet fillings. It is cooked quickly over medium-high heat. The Italian omelette, or frittata, traditionally has the filling ingredients stirred into the eggs. It is cooked slowly over low heat or baked, so it tends to be more firm than a French omelette. It is not folded. The top may be finished under a broiler or the frittata may be flipped to cook the top. A frittata is somewhat similar to a quiche – without the crust – so there are fewer calories.

** If you prefer, use an ovenproof skillet and place under a preheated broiler for a few seconds to set frittata top.

spaghetti omelette

This quick omelette is a great way to use up leftovers.

¼-½ cup leftover spaghetti sauce	50-125 mL	1	Heat the spaghetti sauce in a small saucepan or in the microwave.
4 eggs	4	2	Spray a medium non-stick skillet with cooking spray. Preheat to medium-high.
1 tbsp water	15 mL	3	Whisk eggs and water together.
		4	Pour eggs into hot skillet. As eggs set at the edges, with spatula, gently lift cooked portion to allow uncooked egg to flow underneath. Cook until bottom is set and top is almost set.
		5	Spoon the hot spaghetti sauce over half of the omelette. Fold other half of the omelette over the sauce.
		6	Cut in half to serve.

Makes 2 servings
Preparation: 3 minutes
Cooking: 5 minutes

Nutrients per serving*
Calories: 163   Protein: 12.8 g
Carbohydrate: 3.2 g   Fat: 10.5 g

Frank Bourque
Irishtown, New Brunswick

variations

* The nutrient analysis for this recipe used a marinara (tomato, onion and herb) spaghetti sauce.

A bit of Parmesan cheese sprinkled over the sauce makes this omelette even tastier.

Substitute your favourite tomato salsa for the spaghetti sauce. Eggs and tomatoes have a natural affinity.

puffy* bread omelette

Surround this attractive, mild-tasting puffy omelette with more intense flavours such as crisp bacon, peppery hash browns, spicy salsa or sharp cheese.

1 cup dry bread cubes	250 mL
1½ cups milk	375 mL
3 eggs, separated	3
salt and pepper to taste	
parsley to taste	
1½ tsp cornstarch	7 mL
½ tsp baking powder	2 mL

1 Place dry bread in a bowl. Pour milk over; let soak for a few minutes. Mix well.

2 Stir beaten egg yolks into bread mixture along with salt, pepper, parsley, cornstarch and baking powder. Blend well.

3 Whip egg whites to stiff peaks. Fold into bread mixture.

4 Spray a medium non-stick skillet with cooking spray. Preheat to medium-high.

5 Pour egg mixture into skillet. Smooth top. Lower heat to medium-low.

6 Cover skillet. Cook for 8 to 10 minutes, or until omelette is set and bottom is browned.

7 Cut into 4 wedges. Serve brown side up on warm plates.

Makes 4 servings
Preparation: 10 minutes
Cooking: 10 minutes

Sophie Léveillé
St-Jean-sur-Richelieu, Quebec

Nutrients per serving
Calories: 123   Protein: 8.2 g
Carbohydrate: 9.2 g   Fat: 5.7 g

* A puffy omelette is somewhat similar to a soufflé. Some recipes use two additional egg whites and then omit the baking powder and cornstarch. Some recipes cook the omelette over medium heat until the bottom is just set, then finish the omelette in a pre-heated 375°F (190°C) oven until puffed and just set.

To make a puffy omelette without the dry bread, use 4 to 6 eggs, separated, and only ¼ to ½ cup (50 to 125 mL) of milk.

organic greens & ginger omelette

Fresh ginger adds spicy heat to this omelette.

½ tsp olive oil	2 mL	1
1 garlic clove, minced	1	
1 tsp grated fresh ginger*	5 mL	
2 cups organic spinach, beet greens OR other greens	500 mL	2
4 eggs	4	3
salt and pepper to taste		4

1 Heat oil in a medium non-stick skillet; sauté garlic and ginger over medium heat until soft but not brown, about 2 minutes.

2 Add greens; sauté until greens wilt, 1 to 2 minutes. Set aside.

3 Whisk eggs, salt and pepper in a small bowl.

4 Pour eggs into a preheated, oiled medium non-stick skillet. As eggs set at the edges, with spatula, gently lift cooked portion to allow uncooked egg to flow underneath. Cook until set, 4 to 6 minutes.

5 Spoon the greens mixture over half of the omelette. Fold the omelette in half and transfer to a warm plate. Cut in half to serve.

Makes 2 servings
Preparation: 5 minutes
Cooking: 8 minutes

Valerie Legacy
Mount Pleasant, Ontario

Nutrients per serving
Calories: 171   Protein: 14.0 g
Carbohydrate: 3.4 g   Fat: 11.2 g

* Fresh ginger has a very different flavour from dried, ground ginger. Grown mostly in Jamaica, Africa and Asian countries, it has a pungent aroma and spicy, peppery flavour. Young ginger, with a thin, pale skin, does not need to be peeled.

flash in the pan frittata

Recipes that use leftovers are like getting a free meal!

1 tbsp butter OR margarine	15 mL
2 green onions, finely chopped	2
½ cup leftover cooked vegetables	125 mL
1 cup leftover cooked rice, any variety	250 mL
5-6 eggs	5-6

Makes 4 servings
Preparation: 5 minutes
Cooking: 14 minutes

1 Heat butter in a large non-stick skillet over medium heat. Add green onions and sauté until softened, about 1 minute.

2 Stir in cooked vegetables and rice; cook and stir for 3 minutes, or until heated through.

3 Whisk eggs in a medium bowl until frothy.

4 Pour eggs into skillet over rice and vegetables; cook over medium-low heat until eggs are almost set.

5 Flip frittata over; cook 1 minute longer.**

6 Cut into wedges and serve.

Nutrients per serving*
Calories: 199   Protein: 9.9 g
Carbohydrate: 18.4 g   Fat: 9.2 g

Richard Castor
Sherwood Park, Alberta

* The nutrient analysis for this recipe used mixed vegetables.

** If you prefer, use an ovenproof skillet and place under a preheated broiler for a few seconds to set frittata top.

variations

Splash a little soy sauce on this frittata just before serving.

To make this frittata more heart-healthy, sauté the vegetables and rice in olive or canola oil instead of butter.

broccoli, spinach & parmesan frittata

A sprinkling of chopped fresh parsley just before serving adds great colour and texture.

3 eggs	3
6 egg whites	6
6 tbsp milk	90 mL
¼ cup chopped broccoli*	50 mL
¼ cup chopped spinach	50 mL
1 tbsp chopped chives	15 mL
salt and pepper to taste	
1 tomato, thinly sliced	1
3 tbsp grated Parmesan cheese	45 mL

Makes 2 generous servings
Preparation: 7 minutes
Cooking: 15 minutes

1 Whisk eggs and egg whites with milk, broccoli, spinach, chives, salt and pepper in a medium bowl.

2 Spray a large ovenproof skillet with cooking spray. Preheat to medium.

3 Pour egg mixture into skillet. Cook over medium heat until set, 10 to 12 minutes. (If you wish, cover skillet to shorten cooking time.)

4 Layer tomato slices on top of the frittata. Sprinkle Parmesan cheese over tomatoes.

5 Place under preheated broiler for 3 minutes, or until cheese melts and bubbles.

6 Cut into wedges to serve.

Nutrients per serving
Calories: 119   Protein: 12.9 g
Carbohydrate: 3.7 g   Fat: 5.7 g

Brenda Blake
Toronto, Ontario

* Broccoli, related to cabbage, cauliflower and Brussels sprouts, is high in the antioxidants vitamin C and beta carotene, plus calcium, iron and riboflavin. Choose deep green broccoli with buds that are tightly closed. Fresh broccoli can be stored in the refrigerator for 3 to 5 days.

east coast fiddle

For an East Coast dinner, serve this omelette with broiled fresh Atlantic salmon – it's good and good for you!

4 eggs	4
¼ cup cold water	50 mL
salt and black OR cayenne pepper to taste	
2 tsp butter OR olive oil	10 mL
1 cup steamed fresh fiddleheads	250 mL
¼ cup crumbled feta cheese	50 mL
¼ cup finely chopped softened* sun-dried tomatoes	50 mL
dillweed to taste	

Makes 4 side dish servings
Preparation: 20 minutes**
Cooking: 5 minutes

Nutrients per serving
Calories: 128   Protein: 8.8 g
Carbohydrate: 4.1 g   Fat: 8.7 g

1 Whisk eggs, water, salt and black pepper together. For a spicier flavour, add cayenne pepper.

2 Heat butter or olive oil in a medium non-stick skillet over medium heat.

3 Pour eggs into hot skillet. As eggs set at the edges, use spatula to gently push cooked portions to the centre. Tilt and rotate skillet. Cook until eggs are almost set, about 5 minutes.

4 Top half of the omelette with fiddleheads, cheese, tomatoes and dill. Fold other half over filling.

5 Cut into 4 portions as soon as cheese melts; serve.

Kathy Birch
Fredericton, New Brunswick

variation

Try asparagus instead of fiddleheads when fiddleheads are not available.

* Soften sun-dried tomatoes by soaking in very hot water for 5 minutes, or until softened. Pat dry, chop and use as required.

** Preparation time includes soaking sun-dried tomatoes and steaming fiddleheads.

note

Be sure to clean fiddleheads thoroughly before cooking. Rinse them well in cold water, trim ends and remove any loose brown bits. Failing to do this will result in a very bitter flavour.

my diet breakfast

This quick and easy omelette is low-calorie but satisfying.

1 egg	1	1	Whisk egg and water together in a small bowl.
1 tsp water	5 mL		
2 medium mushrooms, sliced	2	2	Spray a small non-stick skillet with cooking spray. Preheat over medium-high heat.
1 cup lightly packed fresh spinach leaves	250 mL	3	Add mushrooms and spinach. Cook until mushrooms are light brown and spinach wilts.
		4	Pour egg over vegetables in skillet. Continue to cook over medium heat until egg is set. Fold omelette and serve.

Makes 1 serving
Preparation: 3 minutes
Cooking: 2 minutes

Nutrients per serving
Calories: 92   Protein: 8.3 g
Carbohydrate: 3.6 g   Fat: 5.2 g

Carolyn DiPasquale
West Vancouver, British Columbia

"squashed" omelette

This is an ideal way to use leftover squash or sweet potatoes.

2 eggs	2	1	Whisk eggs in a medium bowl.
1/4 cup mashed cooked squash	50 mL	2	Spray a small non-stick skillet with cooking spray. Preheat to medium.
salt and pepper to taste		3	Pour eggs into skillet. As eggs set at the edges, with spatula, gently lift cooked portion to allow uncooked egg to flow underneath. Cook until bottom is set and top is almost set.
		4	Spoon squash along centre of omelette. Season with salt and pepper. Fold both sides of omelette over squash. Serve on a warm plate.

Makes 1 serving
Preparation: 2 minutes
Cooking: 4 minutes

Nutrients per serving
Calories: 177   Protein: 13.0 g
Carbohydrate: 9.0 g   Fat: 10.0 g

Wendy Lott
Peterborough, Ontario

frittata with zing

Basil, peppers, onions, garlic and spicy tomato-clam juice are a zesty combination. For more zing, add green hot pepper sauce and a sprinkle of freshly ground pepper.

1 tsp olive oil	5 mL
1 small onion, minced	1
1 garlic clove*, minced, or more, to taste	1
4 eggs, beaten	4
½ cup chopped green, red OR yellow peppers	125 mL
½ cup chopped tomato	125 mL
chopped fresh basil to taste	
¼ cup spicy tomato-clam juice	50 mL

Makes 2 servings
Preparation: 10 minutes
Cooking: 10 minutes

1 Heat olive oil in a medium non-stick skillet over medium heat.

2 Add onion and sauté until softened, about 2 minutes. Stir in garlic.

3 Stir eggs, chopped vegetables and basil together. Pour over onion in the skillet.

4 Drizzle tomato-clam juice over the frittata.

5 Cook until frittata shrinks and is no longer moist. Lift edges during cooking to allow uncooked egg to flow underneath.

6 Cut in wedges and serve on warm plates.

David McCaughna
Toronto, Ontario

Nutrients per serving
Calories: 203   Protein: 13.7 g
Carbohydrate: 11.7 g   Fat: 11.3 g

* Olympic athletes in ancient Greece and slaves building the pyramids in Egypt ate garlic for physical strength. Garlic has also long been promoted for its many health benefits, from use as an antiseptic to alleviating breathing difficulties to lowering cholesterol and warding off vampires! A member of the lily family, it is related to onions, leeks, chives and shallots.

pineapple & tofu omelette

A delicious way to include healthy, low-fat soy/tofu in your diet.

¼ cup chicken stock	50 mL	
¼ red pepper, chopped	¼	
¼ onion, chopped	¼	
2 tbsp firm tofu*, crumbled	30 mL	
2 eggs	2	
2 tbsp water	30 mL	
salt and pepper to taste		
2 tbsp finely chopped pineapple	30 mL	
½ slice fat-free Cheddar cheese	½	

1. Bring chicken stock to a boil in a small saucepan. Add red pepper, onion and tofu; simmer until tender, about 5 minutes. Drain well.

2. Whisk eggs, water, salt and pepper in a small bowl.

3. Spray a small non-stick skillet with cooking spray. Preheat to medium-hot.

4. Pour eggs into skillet. As eggs set at the edges, with spatula, gently lift cooked portion to allow uncooked egg to flow underneath. Cook until bottom is set and top is almost set.

5. Spoon tofu mixture, pineapple and cheese over half of the omelette. Fold other half over filling.

6. Slide the omelette onto a warm plate.

Makes 1 serving
Preparation: 8 minutes
Cooking: 8 minutes

Nutrients per serving
Calories: 224   Protein: 18.8 g
Carbohydrate: 11.7 g   Fat: 11.6 g

Kim Pickup
Lower Sackville, Nova Scotia

* Tofu is available in soft to extra-firm textures. It is made from soy milk in a process similar to making cheese. Store tofu, refrigerated, for no more than 1 week, once opened. Cover with water and change the water daily. It may be frozen for up to 3 months. Protein-rich tofu is also low in calories and fat.

smoked salmon delight

Eggs and smoked salmon are a great combination.
This simple omelette is surprising and delicious.

2 oz smoked salmon, chopped	60 g	1
1 small tomato, chopped	1	
1 green onion, chopped	1	
2 mushrooms, chopped	2	
¼ tsp nutmeg	1 mL	
¼ tsp curry powder	1 mL	
4 eggs	4	

Makes 2 servings
Preparation: 10 minutes
Cooking: 6 minutes

1. Combine smoked salmon, tomato, green onion and mushrooms in a small bowl. Mix in spices. Let stand for 5 minutes to blend flavours.

2. Whisk eggs in another small bowl.

3. Spray a medium non-stick skillet with cooking spray. Preheat to medium.

4. Pour eggs into skillet. As eggs set at the edges, with spatula, gently lift cooked portion to allow uncooked egg to flow underneath. Cook until bottom is set and top is almost set.

5. Spread salmon mixture over half of the omelette. Fold other half over filling.

6. Cut in half to serve.

Nutrients per serving
Calories: 197   Protein: 18.6 g
Carbohydrate: 4.3 g   Fat: 11.5 g

Peter Dielissen
Fredericton, New Brunswick

note

Because the smoked salmon mixture isn't cooked, after adding it to the omelette you may want to cover the skillet and leave for 2 minutes to warm the filling.

black bean & salsa omelette

For the most flavour, choose spicy salsa. This healthy omelette looks and tastes great!

¼ cup cooked black beans* (rinse and drain if using canned black beans)	50 mL	
¼ cup salsa	50 mL	
2 tbsp chopped sun-dried tomatoes**	30 mL	
2 eggs	2	
1 tbsp milk	15 mL	
salt and pepper to taste		

Makes 1 serving
Preparation: 8 minutes
Cooking: 5 minutes

Nutrients per serving
Calories: 234   Protein: 17.6 g
Carbohydrate: 17.5 g   Fat: 10.7 g

1 Combine black beans, salsa and sun-dried tomatoes in a small bowl. Set aside.

2 Whisk eggs with milk, salt and pepper in another small bowl.

3 Spray a medium non-stick skillet with cooking spray. Preheat to medium.

4 Pour eggs into hot skillet. As eggs set at the edges, with spatula, gently lift cooked portion to allow uncooked egg to flow underneath. Cook until bottom is set and top is almost set.

5 Spoon bean mixture down centre of omelette. Fold both sides over filling.

Colya Kaminiarz
Vancouver, British Columbia

* Black beans, also called turtle beans, have a slightly sweet, nutty flavour. They have long been used in Caribbean, South American, Mexican and Asian dishes such as rich, earthy black bean soups and spicy black bean sauces. Like other dried beans, black beans have a high protein, iron, calcium and phosphorus content.

** Soften sun-dried tomatoes by soaking in very hot water for 5 minutes, or until softened. Pat dry, chop and use as required.

zesty omelette *with salsa*

This omelette is quick, simple and tasty.

2 eggs	2
2 tbsp milk	30 mL
2 tsp onion soup mix	10 mL
2 tsp salsa*	10 mL

Makes 1 serving
Preparation: 2 minutes
Cooking: 5 minutes

Nutrients per serving
Calories: 187   Protein: 14.4 g
Carbohydrate: 7.0 g   Fat: 11.0 g

1 Whisk eggs, milk and soup mix in a small bowl.

2 Spray a small non-stick skillet with cooking spray. Preheat over medium-high heat.

3 Pour egg mixture into skillet. Cook until eggs are set, 3 to 4 minutes, lifting edges during cooking to allow uncooked egg to flow underneath.

4 Spoon salsa over omelette. Cover skillet briefly to warm salsa.

5 Serve on a warm plate.

Penny Horvath
North Vancouver, British Columbia

* Salsa is Spanish for sauce. Fresh or cooked and processed salsas may include chopped tomatoes, garlic, onions and herbs, or may involve a variety of diced fruits, with or without tomatoes. Minced jalapeños are often an ingredient.

thai stuffed omelette

Serve this omelette with hot sauce if you don't have a fresh hot red chili.
The chili hit really makes this omelette shine.

1 firm tomato, chopped	1	
½ small green pepper, chopped	½	
1 small onion, chopped	1	
2 tsp oil, divided	10 mL	
½ cup minced lean pork, about 4 oz (125 g)	125 mL	
½ cup green peas	125 mL	
1 tsp fish sauce	5 mL	
¼ tsp white pepper	1 mL	
¼ tsp soy sauce	1 mL	
3 eggs, beaten	3	
coriander leaves to taste		
1 small hot red chili pepper, thinly sliced	1	

1. Combine tomato, green pepper and onion in a small bowl.

2. Heat 1 tsp (5 mL) oil in a wok over high heat. Add pork; fry and stir for 2 minutes.

3. Stir tomato mixture into pork along with peas, fish sauce, pepper and soy sauce. Cook and stir for 5 to 8 minutes, or until pork is fully cooked and mixture thickens. Taste and add more soy sauce and salt if needed.

4. Heat remaining oil in a small non-stick skillet. When skillet is hot, pour in ¼ of the eggs.

5. Rotate skillet so egg mixture coats bottom. Cook until eggs are set. Slide omelette onto a warm plate.

6. Spoon ¼ of pork mixture into centre of omelette. Fold 2 opposite sides of omelette to the centre, then fold in the 2 remaining sides so that a square is formed.

7. Use the same procedure to prepare 3 more omelettes.

8. Place omelettes on individual plates. Garnish with coriander leaves and red chili to taste. Serve with rice.

Makes 4 servings
Preparation: 7 minutes
Cooking: 15 minutes

Nutrients per serving
Calories: 166   Protein: 11.6 g
Carbohydrate: 6.5 g   Fat: 10.4 g

Bill Friedman
Toronto, Ontario

fisherman's frittata

A crisp cucumber salad is perfect with this brunch or dinner frittata.

1 trout fillet, about 6 oz (150 g), cooked	1
6 eggs	6
½ cup milk	125 mL
¼ cup chopped parsley*	50 mL
salt to taste	

1. Cut trout into bite-sized pieces.

2. Whisk eggs and milk together. Stir in trout. Add parsley and salt.

3. Spray a large non-stick skillet with cooking spray. Preheat over medium-high heat.

4. Pour egg mixture into skillet. As mixture sets at the edges, with spatula, gently lift cooked portion to allow uncooked egg to flow underneath. Cook until bottom is set and top is almost set.

5. Slide frittata onto a plate. Flip back into skillet. Return to burner briefly to finish cooking.**

6. Cut frittata into 4 wedges and serve.

Makes 4 servings
Preparation: 15 minutes
Cooking: 12 minutes

Claire Martel
Jonquière, Quebec

Nutrients per serving
Calories: 181   Protein: 18.4 g
Carbohydrate: 2.1 g   Fat: 10.4 g

* Curly-leaf and flat-leaf (Italian) parsley are the most popular of the more than 30 varieties of parsley available. Although most often used as a garnish in North American dishes, peppery-flavoured parsley is nutritious, rich in vitamins A and C. Middle Eastern recipes such as Tabbouleh, Hummus and Baba Ghanouj feature parsley, as do many Italian, Greek and French dishes.

** If you prefer, use an ovenproof skillet and place under a preheated broiler for a few seconds to set frittata top.

apple, gruyère & prosciutto omelette, page 39

breakfast
& brunch

sure wake-up omelette

Pungent and spicy, horseradish adds a real kick to this imaginative flavour combination.

2 eggs	2	
1 tbsp milk	15 mL	
1 tbsp EACH minced red and green peppers	15 mL	
salt and pepper to taste		
horseradish* to taste		
1 tbsp shredded Cheddar cheese	15 mL	

Makes 1 serving
Preparation: 4 minutes
Cooking: 4 minutes

1 Whisk eggs and milk in a medium bowl. Stir in peppers, salt, pepper and horseradish.

2 Spray a small non-stick skillet with cooking spray. Preheat to medium.

3 Pour egg mixture into skillet. As mixture sets at the edges, with spatula, gently lift cooked portion to allow uncooked egg to flow underneath. Cook until bottom is set and top is almost set, about 4 minutes.

4 Sprinkle cheese on top. Fold the omelette in half.

5 Slide onto a warm plate.

Nutrients per serving
Calories: 186   Protein: 14.7 g
Carbohydrate: 2.6 g   Fat: 12.6 g

Aleksandra Froncisz
London, Ontario

* Try 2 to 3 tsp (10 to 15 mL) of horseradish if you really want to taste it. Traditionally one of the five bitter herbs of the Passover, horseradish adds zest to meats, seafood and fish. It is available fresh, bottled (prepared) and dried. Prepared white horseradish is preserved in vinegar and the red version is preserved in beet juice.

open-faced veggie frittata

This frittata is very versatile – try it with your favourite vegetable combinations.

1 tbsp vegetable oil	15 mL	
½ cup EACH chopped onion, green pepper and mushrooms	125 mL	
1 garlic clove, minced	1	
¼ cup chopped softened sun-dried tomatoes*	50 mL	
3 eggs	3	
½ cup milk	125 mL	
salt and pepper to taste		
½ cup your favourite shredded cheese	125 mL	

Makes 2 servings
Preparation: 12 minutes
Cooking: 15 minutes

Nutrients per serving
Calories: 364   Protein: 20.6 g
Carbohydrate: 15.2 g Fat: 25.2 g

1. Heat oil in a medium skillet. Add onion, peppers, mushrooms, garlic and tomatoes. Sauté until tender.

2. Beat eggs, milk, salt and pepper together in a small bowl. Pour over vegetable mixture in skillet.

3. Cover skillet. Cook frittata over medium-low heat for 8 to 12 minutes, or until set. Loosen frittata from skillet by sliding spatula under edges.

4. Slide frittata onto a heatproof plate. Invert skillet over the plate; flip so frittata drops back into skillet.**

5. Sprinkle cheese over frittata. Cover skillet until cheese melts. Cut frittata in wedges to serve.

Derrick Logan
Halifax, Nova Scotia

* Soften sun-dried tomatoes by soaking in very hot water for 5 minutes, or until softened. Pat dry, chop and use as required.

** If you prefer, use an ovenproof skillet and place under a preheated broiler for a few seconds to set frittata top.

omelette olé

Rise and shine to these spicy Mexican flavours.

4 eggs	4
2 tbsp chopped green chilies	30 mL
2 tbsp chopped green olives	30 mL
2 tsp butter OR margarine	10 mL
¼ cup shredded Cheddar cheese	50 mL
salsa to taste	

Makes 2 servings
Preparation: 6 minutes
Cooking: 7 minutes

1. Whisk eggs in a medium bowl. Stir in chilies and olives; mix well.

2. Melt butter in a hot 10" (25 cm) skillet.

3. Pour egg mixture into skillet. As mixture sets at the edges, with spatula, gently lift cooked portion and tilt skillet to allow uncooked egg to flow underneath. Cook until bottom is set and top is almost set.

4. Sprinkle cheese over half of omelette. Fold other half over.

5. Cut omelette in half and slide onto warm plates. Top with salsa.

Nutrients per serving
Calories: 250   Protein: 16.2 g
Carbohydrate: 1.8 g   Fat: 19.6 g

Carolann Westbrook
Brantford, Ontario

cilantro & lemon omelette

A must for those who love the distinctive flavour of cilantro.

5 eggs, beaten	5	
2 tbsp milk	30 mL	
¼ cup chopped fresh cilantro leaves*	50 mL	
2 tsp fresh lemon juice	10 mL	
salt and pepper to taste		

1. Whisk all ingredients together in a medium bowl.

2. Spray a medium non-stick skillet with cooking spray. Preheat to medium.

3. Pour egg mixture into skillet. As mixture sets at the edges, with spatula, gently lift cooked portion to allow uncooked egg to flow underneath. Continue cooking until omelette is fluffy and cooked through.

4. Fold omelette in half and cut in half. Remove from the skillet.

5. Sprinkle with additional chopped cilantro and serve.

Makes 2 servings
Preparation: 6 minutes
Cooking: 8 minutes

Nutrients per serving
Calories: 191   Protein: 16.0 g
Carbohydrate: 2.0 g   Fat: 12.7 g

Tara Mitrovka
Verdun, Quebec

* Cilantro (coriander, Chinese parsley) is widely used in Asia and the Mediterranean. The leaves have a pungent flavour that goes well with spicy dishes. To store in the refrigerator, place stems in water and loosely cover leaves with a plastic bag. Change water daily. Coriander seeds have a lemony caraway flavour and are used in pickling, curries and baking.

asparagus, avocado & grapefruit omelette

This eclectic assortment of ingredients is surprising and delicious.

4 eggs	4
salt and pepper to taste	
4 stalks asparagus, lightly steamed	4
1 avocado *, peeled, chopped	1
½ pink grapefruit, cut into small chunks	½
⅓ cup grated smoked Gruyère cheese	75 mL
chopped fresh herbs to taste (your choice)	

Makes 2 servings
Preparation: 12 minutes
Cooking: 6 minutes

1. Whisk eggs in a small bowl. Add salt and pepper.

2. Spray a medium non-stick skillet with cooking spray. Heat until hot.

3. Pour eggs into skillet. As eggs set at the edges, with spatula, gently lift cooked portion to allow uncooked egg to flow underneath. Cook until bottom is set and top is almost set.

4. Spoon remaining ingredients over half of the omelette. Continue cooking until cheese melts.

5. Fold the omelette in half. Cut in 2 portions and serve.

Nutrients per serving
Calories: 482   Protein: 26.2 g
Carbohydrate: 14.2 g Fat: 37.1 g

Darian Tamlin
Montreal, Quebec

* Avocados have a rich nutty flavour and creamy texture. Also called alligator pears, they range in size from 1 ounce (30 g) to 4 pounds (2 kg) and ripen best off the tree. To ripen avocados, place several avocados in a paper bag at room temperature for 2 to 3 days. Refrigerate ripe avocados. Dipping cut avocado in lemon or lime juice helps prevent discolouration.

cashew & spinach fiesta frittata

Cashews add crunch and a rich buttery flavour to this open-faced spinach frittata.
The orange and cucumber garnish is fresh tasting and colourful.

3 eggs	3	1	Whisk eggs, milk, hot pepper sauce, salt and pepper in a small bowl.
½ cup milk OR cream	125 mL		
½ tsp hot pepper sauce	2 mL	2	Heat oil over medium heat in a medium non-stick ovenproof skillet. Add cashews and sauté.
salt and pepper to taste			
1 tsp vegetable oil	5 mL	3	Stir in green onion and spinach; cook and stir until aromatic. Spread vegetables in an even layer in the skillet.
¼ cup chopped cashews	50 mL		
chopped green onion to taste			
1 cup fresh spinach leaves	250 mL	4	Pour egg mixture over vegetables. Cook until eggs are almost set.
½ cup grated Swiss cheese	125 mL	5	Sprinkle cheese over frittata. Place in a preheated 375°F (190°C) oven until cheese melts and frittata is set.
English cucumber slices for garnish		6	Cut the frittata into wedges. Garnish each serving with cucumber and orange slices.
orange slices for garnish			

Makes 3 servings
Preparation: 10 minutes
Cooking: 12 minutes

Nutrients per serving
Calories: 248   Protein: 15.3 g
Carbohydrate: 7.5 g   Fat: 17.8 g

Jason Young
Halifax, Nova Scotia

note

By substituting milk for cream, and reducing the amount from ½ cup (125 mL) to ¼ cup (50 mL), this frittata is heart healthier and still delicious.

apple, gruyère & prosciutto omelette

The subtle sweetness of the apple is a perfect complement to the salty meat and creamy cheese in this omelette filling.

1 tbsp butter	15 mL	1	Melt butter in a heavy, medium, non-stick skillet.
1 large sweet apple, grated	1		
¼ cup thinly sliced onion	50 mL	2	Sauté apple and onion over medium heat until onion is translucent. Remove from skillet.
4 eggs	4		
2 tsp water	10 mL	3	Whisk together eggs, water and parsley.
1 tbsp minced parsley	15 mL		
2 oz Gruyère OR Swiss cheese, grated	60 g	4	Spray skillet with cooking spray.
		5	Pour egg mixture into hot skillet. As mixture sets at the edges, with spatula, gently lift cooked portion to allow uncooked egg to flow underneath. Cook until bottom is set and top is almost set.
2 oz thinly sliced prosciutto, slivered	60 g		
salt and pepper to taste			

Makes 2 servings
Preparation: 10 minutes
Cooking: 8 minutes

6   Place apple mixture on half of the omelette. Top with cheese, prosciutto, salt and pepper. Fold and serve.

Nutrients per serving
Calories: 406   Protein: 26.4 g
Carbohydrate: 13.3 g   Fat: 27.5 g

Nancy MacLeod
Halifax, Nova Scotia

sunday morning bliss

*Satisfying and substantial, this combination of
flavours and textures is ideal for a hearty brunch.*

5 eggs	5	1	Beat eggs and milk in a medium bowl.
1 tsp milk	5 mL	2	Stir tomato, bacon and pepper into eggs.
½ medium tomato, diced	½		
3 strips bacon, cooked, crumbled	3	3	Heat oil in a non-stick skillet, or spray with cooking spray. Set to medium heat. Sauté onion until translucent.
pepper to taste			
1 tsp olive oil (optional)	5 mL	4	Pour egg mixture over onion. Cook over medium heat without stirring, lifting edges to allow uncooked egg to flow underneath. Continue cooking until bottom is set and top is almost set.
½ medium onion, diced	½		
¼ cup herbed cream cheese	50 mL		

5 Scatter small spoonfuls of cream cheese over half of the omelette. Fold other half over to cover cheese. Let stand until cheese melts.

Makes 2 servings
Preparation: 10 minutes
Cooking: 12 minutes

6 Cut omelette in half. Serve with toast and chunky hash brown potatoes.

Nutrients per serving
Calories: 349   Protein: 20.6 g
Carbohydrate: 6.3 g   Fat: 26.3 g

Jennifer Hardy
Burnaby, British Columbia

pineapple & ham omelette

Ham and pineapple seem to be made for one another.
This sweet/salty flavour combo is even better with two kinds of cheese.

6 eggs	6	
6 tbsp water	90 mL	
salt and pepper to taste		
½ cup pineapple tidbits	125 mL	
½ cup diced ham	125 mL	
½ cup grated Monterey Jack cheese	125 mL	
½ cup grated Cheddar cheese	125 mL	

Makes 3 servings
Preparation: 8 minutes
Cooking: 10 minutes

1. Whisk eggs, water, salt and pepper in a medium bowl.

2. Spray a large non-stick skillet with cooking spray. Preheat to medium-hot.

3. Pour egg mixture into skillet. As mixture sets at the edges, with spatula, gently lift cooked portion to allow uncooked egg to flow underneath. Cook until bottom is set and top is almost set.

4. When eggs are almost set, sprinkle the remaining ingredients over half of the omelette.

5. Fold other half of the omelette over filling. Continue cooking until cheese melts, about 2 minutes.

6. Cut the omelette into 3 portions. Serve on warm plates.

Kerry Strain
Campbell River, British Columbia

Nutrients per serving
Calories: 338   Protein: 26.2 g
Carbohydrate: 5.4 g   Fat: 23.0 g

tomato & bacon omelette

Dijon and Cheddar add zest – this attractive omelette tastes as good as it looks.

4 eggs, separated	4	1	Whisk egg yolks, mustard, salt and pepper in a medium bowl.
2 tsp Dijon mustard	10 mL		
salt and pepper to taste		2	Beat egg whites in a separate bowl until soft peaks form.
½ cup chopped tomatoes, drained	125 mL	3	Fold whites into yolks.
½ cup chopped, cooked bacon (5 to 6 slices)	125 mL	4	Spray a non-stick skillet with cooking spray. Preheat to medium.
½ cup grated Cheddar cheese	125 mL	5	Pour eggs into skillet. Arrange tomatoes and bacon over omelette. Cover skillet; cook over medium-low heat until eggs are set, 8 to 9 minutes.

Makes 2 servings
Preparation: 11 minutes
Cooking: 10 minutes

6 Top omelette with cheese and fold in half. Cut in 2 portions and serve.

Nutrients per serving
Calories: 388   Protein: 26.2 g
Carbohydrate: 3.5 g   Fat: 29.5 g

Wayne Colborne
Truro, Nova Scotia

cheese & bacon frittata

So tasty, it's possible that this frittata may serve only two or three.

6 eggs	6	1	Whisk eggs and sour cream. Stir in cheese and bacon.
2 tbsp sour cream	30 mL		
2 tbsp grated cheese	30 mL	2	Spray a medium non-stick skillet with cooking spray. Preheat until hot.
2-3 tbsp crumbled bacon	30-45 mL	3	Pour egg mixture into skillet. As mixture sets at the edges, gently lift cooked portion to allow uncooked egg to flow underneath. Cook until bottom is set and top is almost set.

Makes 4 servings
Preparation: 5 minutes
Cooking: 10 minutes

4 Cut into wedges and serve.

Nutrients per serving
Calories: 148   Protein: 11.1 g
Carbohydrate: 0.8 g   Fat: 10.8 g

Edward Kennedy
Sydney, Nova Scotia

layered mushroom, zucchini & pepper omelette

*This beautiful layered omelette is a bit of work,
but try it for a weekend brunch with your family or guests helping out.*

1 cup sliced mushrooms, sautéed until golden with 1 tbsp (15 mL) olive oil	250 mL	
1 cup chopped zucchini, steamed or sautéed	250 mL	
1 cup chopped red pepper, sautéed until soft with 2 tbsp (30 mL) chopped onion	250 mL	
4 slices bacon, chopped, cooked until crisp	4	
salt and pepper to taste		
10 eggs	10	
5 tbsp water	75 mL	
1⅓ cups your favourite shredded cheese	325 mL	

Makes 4 to 6 servings
Preparation: 15 minutes
Cooking/Assembly: 35 minutes

1. Season mushrooms, zucchini, peppers and bacon with salt and pepper. Keep warm in separate bowls in a 200°F (100°C) oven.

2. Whisk 2 eggs with 1 tbsp (15 mL) water in a small bowl.

3. Spray a medium non-stick skillet with cooking spray. Preheat to medium.

4. Pour eggs into skillet. As eggs set at the edges, with spatula, gently lift cooked portion to allow uncooked egg to flow underneath. Cook until bottom is set and top is almost set.

5. Slide the omelette onto a large oven-proof plate. Spoon the mushrooms evenly over the omelette. Sprinkle ⅓ cup (75 mL) of cheese over filling. Place in oven to keep warm.

6. Prepare 4 more 2-egg omelettes using the same technique as above. As each omelette is cooked, set it in place on top of the previous omelette and filling, adding the next layer of filling and ⅓ cup (75 mL) of cheese each time.

7. Set the final omelette in place on top of the stack, browned side up.

8. Cut into wedges to serve.

Nutrients per serving
Calories: 281   Protein: 18.4 g
Carbohydrate: 4.3 g   Fat: 21.0 g

Monique Beauchemin Beaudry
Granby, Quebec

maple syrup & bacon frittata

Maple syrup, bacon and pineapple are a luscious combination.
Fruit and flowers make a beautiful presentation.

4 eggs	4	
1 tbsp milk	15 mL	
1 tbsp maple syrup, or more, to taste	15 mL	
¼ cup drained, crushed pineapple	50 mL	
4 slices cooked back bacon, slivered	4	
1 medium tomato, chopped	1	
chopped rosemary and parsley to taste		
salt and pepper to taste		
seasonal fresh fruit and edible flowers*		

1 Beat eggs, milk and maple syrup together in a medium bowl. Stir in pineapple, bacon, tomato, herbs and seasonings.

2 Spray a large non-stick skillet with cooking spray. Preheat to medium.

3 Pour egg mixture into skillet. As mixture sets at the edges, with spatula, gently lift cooked portion to allow uncooked egg to flow underneath. Cook until bottom is set and top is almost set.

4 Cover the skillet for the final few minutes of cooking.

5 Cut the frittata into wedges. Garnish with fruit and serve on a bed of edible flowers.

Makes 2 servings
Preparation: 10 minutes
Cooking: 8 minutes

Nutrients per serving
Calories: 290   Protein: 24.5 g
Carbohydrate: 15.6 g Fat: 14.1 g

Richard Hall
Surrey, British Columbia

* Edible flowers include peppery nasturtiums, geraniums, pansies, carnations, marigolds, chive blossoms, peonies, roses, violas, squash and zucchini blossoms, snapdragons, tulips and more. Before using edible flowers, make sure that they have NOT been sprayed with insecticides.

¡hola mexico!
page 58

curry-lime omelette

Curry powder and cumin add rich colour and flavour to this exotic omelette.
Mango chutney complements it beautifully.

6 eggs	6
1 medium tomato, seeded, chopped	1
¼ cup chopped cilantro	50 mL
4 mushrooms, chopped	4
3 tbsp chopped red onion	45 mL
3 garlic cloves, chopped	3
2 tsp lime juice	10 mL
1½ tsp curry powder*	7 mL
1 tsp red pepper flakes, or less, to taste	5 mL
½ tsp ground cumin	2 mL
salt and pepper to taste	
2 tsp vegetable oil	10 mL
1 medium tomato, sliced	1
¼ cup shredded old Cheddar cheese	50 mL

Makes 3 servings
Preparation: 12 minutes
Cooking: 12 minutes

1 Whisk eggs in a medium bowl.

2 Stir in tomato, cilantro, mushrooms, onion, garlic, lime juice, curry powder, red pepper flakes, cumin, salt and pepper.

3 Heat oil in a medium non-stick skillet.

4 Pour egg mixture into skillet. As mixture sets at the edges, with spatula, gently lift cooked portion to let uncooked egg flow underneath. Cover and cook until eggs are almost set and bubbles start appearing. Bottom of omelette should be brown at this point.

5 Top half of the omelette with tomato slices and cheese. Cook 2 more minutes, or until cheese melts.

6 Fold the omelette and cook for another few minutes.

7 Cut into 3 portions and slide onto warm plates. Garnish with your choice of chopped cilantro, chopped tomato, or mango or lime chutney.

Mou Mukherjee
Toronto, Ontario

Nutrients per serving
Calories: 216   Protein: 16.2 g
Carbohydrate: 7.8 g   Fat: 13.6 g

* Curry powder is a blend of up to 20 ground herbs, seeds and spices. Indian cooks usually blend their own curry powders which vary from cook to cook and region to region. Madras is the hottest of the commercial powders. Store in an airtight container for up to 2 months.

roasted red pepper, feta & artichoke frittata

Serve this frittata with focaccia bread and a Caesar salad for a quick and easy dinner.

1 tbsp butter	15 mL	
1 garlic clove, minced	1	
4 eggs	4	
¼ cup crumbled feta cheese	50 mL	
¼ cup chopped, roasted red peppers*	50 mL	
4 artichoke hearts, chopped	4	
salt and pepper to taste		
6 Kalamata olives, chopped	6	
grated Parmesan cheese		

Makes 2 servings
Preparation: 5 minutes
Cooking: 12 minutes

1 Melt butter over medium-low heat in a medium non-stick skillet. When froth subsides, add garlic. Sauté gently.

2 Whisk eggs in a medium bowl. Stir in feta, peppers and artichokes. Season with salt and pepper.

3 Pour egg mixture into skillet. Cover and cook for 8 to 10 minutes, or until eggs are set on the bottom but still moist on top.

4 Sprinkle olives and Parmesan cheese over the frittata. If the skillet is oven-proof, place it under the broiler briefly, until the eggs are almost set. Do not overcook. If the skillet is not ovenproof, cover it to melt the cheese. The frittata should be firm but not dry and the Parmesan cheese should be just melted, not browned.

5 Cut the frittata in wedges and serve.

JoAnne Dooley
Surrey, British Columbia

Nutrients per serving
Calories: 312   Protein: 18.0 g
Carbohydrate: 13.3 g Fat: 21.7 g

* To roast red peppers, place halved peppers cut side down on a baking sheet. Roast at 400°F (200°C) for 15 to 20 minutes, or until peppers are soft. Place peppers in a bowl and cover until cool, then peel. Peppers may also be broiled or barbecued until the skin blisters and turns black – watch carefully.

Leftovers can be layered with waxed paper and frozen for future use.

Bottles of roasted red peppers are available in many supermarkets.

falafel omoletta

Falafel mix adds crunchy texture and spicy flavour to this Middle Eastern-inspired omelette. You could also stir the steamed vegetables into the egg mixture before cooking to create a frittata version.

3 eggs	3
2 tbsp water	30 mL
3-4 tbsp falafel mix*	45-60 mL
½ cup EACH lightly steamed broccoli and cauliflower	125 mL
handful of raisins	
salt and pepper to taste	

Makes 1 generous serving
Preparation: 8 minutes
Cooking: 8 minutes

1 Whisk eggs, water and the falafel mix together in a small bowl.

2 Spray a medium non-stick skillet with cooking spray. Heat until hot.

3 Pour egg mixture into skillet. As mixture sets at the edges, with spatula, gently lift edges of omelette to let uncooked egg flow underneath.

4 Flip omelette like a pancake to cook the other side. Spoon broccoli, cauliflower and raisins over half of omelette. Sprinkle with salt and pepper.

5 Fold omelette over filling. Serve on warm plates.

Nutrients per serving
Calories: 559   Protein: 31.5 g
Carbohydrate: 81.3 g Fat: 16.5 g

Monique Lirette
Calgary, Alberta

* Falafels are small deep-fried balls of spiced ground chickpeas mixed with onion, garlic, cumin, coriander, cayenne, etc. These savoury Middle Eastern specialties are becoming popular throughout North America. Falafel mix is available in most large supermarkets.

nutty green omelette

This unusual flavour combination – toasted pine nuts, spinach and sweet, spicy hoisin sauce – really works.

¼ cup pine nuts	50 mL	
3-4 eggs	3-4	
1 tbsp hoisin sauce*	15 mL	
1 tbsp water	15 mL	
2 cups shredded fresh spinach	500 mL	

1 Toast pine nuts in a medium-hot non-stick large skillet for about 3 minutes, or until nicely browned. Remove; set aside and keep warm.

2 Spray the same skillet with cooking spray. Preheat to medium.

3 Beat eggs with hoisin sauce and water.

4 Pour egg mixture into hot skillet. As mixture sets at the edges, with spatula, gently lift cooked portion to let uncooked egg flow underneath. Cook until bottom is set and top is almost set.

5 Sprinkle spinach and pine nuts over omelette. Fold omelette in half. Cook 1 to 2 minutes more to wilt spinach.

6 Cut omelette in half. Transfer to warm plates and serve.

Makes 2 servings
Preparation: 6 minutes
Cooking: 12 minutes

Nutrients per serving
Calories: 253   Protein: 16.0 g
Carbohydrate: 8.9 g   Fat: 18.1 g

Denise Lauzon
Duncan, British Columbia

* A blend of spices, soybeans, garlic and hot peppers, hoisin sauce is used in Chinese cooking with meats and shellfish. Often called Peking sauce, it has a rich red/brown colour. Available in most supermarkets, hoisin sauce should be refrigerated once it is opened.

potato & jalapeño omelette

Potato Tortilla (omelette), a classic Spanish dish, is served hot or at room temperature. Each household and tapas bar has its own recipe. These omelettes/frittatas have a lower ratio of eggs to filling than traditional omelettes. The mint is a surprise, but it works!

2 eggs	**2**
1 cooked potato, sliced	**1**
1 tbsp chopped fresh mint	**15 mL**
¼ cup grated cheese	**50 mL**
2 mushrooms, chopped	**2**
1 jalapeño, thinly sliced	**1**
pepper to taste	

1 Whisk eggs in a medium bowl. Stir in remaining ingredients.

2 Spray a medium skillet with cooking spray. Preheat to medium.

3 Pour egg mixture into skillet. Cover and cook for 6 to 8 minutes, or until set.

4 Cut in half and serve with medium-hot fresh salsa.

Makes 2 servings
Preparation: 5 minutes
Cooking: 8 minutes

Nutrients per serving
Calories: 236   Protein: 14.6 g
Carbohydrate: 16.7 g Fat: 12.3 g

Noorani Kauser
North York, Ontario

greek omelette with basil pesto

The heavenly combination of pesto and tomatoes is even better with feta cheese and Greek olives. Making one large omelette in a medium skillet and cutting it in half to serve would shorten the cooking time.

½ onion, chopped	½
½ green pepper, chopped	½
1 tbsp pesto sauce *, or more, to taste	15 mL
1 tomato, chopped, drained	1
4 eggs	4
4 tbsp water	60 mL
salt and pepper to taste	
¼ cup crumbled feta cheese	50 mL
¼ cup chopped Kalamata olives	50 mL

Makes 2 servings
Preparation: 8 minutes
Cooking: 15 minutes

1. Spray a small non-stick skillet with cooking spray. Sauté onion and peppers for 2 minutes. Stir in pesto sauce and tomatoes; set aside.

2. Beat 2 eggs with 2 tbsp (30 mL) of water. Season with salt and pepper.

3. Spray the same skillet with cooking spray. Preheat to medium.

4. Pour egg mixture into skillet. As mixture sets at the edges, with spatula, gently lift cooked portion to allow uncooked egg to flow underneath. Cook until bottom is set and top is almost set.

5. Spoon half of the pesto mixture over half of the omelette. Add half of the feta cheese and olives.

6. Fold the omelette; transfer to a plate and keep warm.

7. Prepare a second omelette using the remaining ingredients.

Linda Mervyn
Kelowna, British Columbia

Nutrients per serving
Calories: 303   Protein: 16.7 g
Carbohydrate: 9.7 g   Fat: 22.5 g

* Pesto, originating in Genoa, Italy, is a blend of fresh basil, garlic, pine nuts, olive oil and Parmesan cheese. Homemade pesto has a fabulous fresh flavour, but acceptable bottled versions are available year round in most supermarkets.

pass da pasta omelette

A crisp, green salad with a tart vinaigrette would be ideal with this hearty omelette.

½ cup Italian tomato sauce	125 mL
3 eggs	3
2 tbsp water	30 mL
salt to taste	
1 cup cooked small pasta* (macaroni, small shells, etc.)	250 mL
½ cup shredded Mozzarella, white Cheddar OR Monterey Jack cheese	125 mL
1 tbsp minced fresh herbs (basil, parsley, thyme, etc.)	15 mL

Makes 1 to 2 servings
Preparation: 6 minutes
Cooking: 8 minutes

1 Heat tomato sauce in a small saucepan or in a microwave; keep warm while preparing omelette.

2 Beat eggs lightly with water and salt.

3 Spray a medium skillet with cooking spray. Preheat to medium.

4 Pour eggs into hot skillet. Distribute pasta evenly over eggs. Gently push mixture from the edges to the centre as the edges set. Cook until omelette is almost set but is still very moist.

5 Sprinkle cheese over the omelette. Fold gently in half.

6 Slide the omelette onto a serving plate. Spoon hot tomato sauce over the omelette.

7 Sprinkle with chopped herbs.

Nutrients per serving
Calories: 317   Protein: 19.5 g
Carbohydrate: 25.5 g Fat: 15.0 g

Marina Latulippe
Ladysmith, British Columbia

* Hundreds of pasta shapes, colours and sizes are available. Children and adults love the unusual shapes, which are also ideal for scooping up flavourful sauces. Some of the more popular small shapes are shells (*conchiglie*), butterflies or bows (*farfalli*), corkscrews (*fusilli*), twists (*gemelli*), cartwheels (*rotelle*), little ears (*orecchiette*) and radiators (*radiatore*).

¡hola mexico!

¡Muy bueno! For a superb zesty flavour, look for canned refried beans with added jalapeño peppers. They work very well in this omelette.

4 eggs	4	
2 tsp water	10 mL	
salt and pepper to taste		
¼ cup refried beans*, heated	50 mL	
¼ cup shredded Monterey Jack cheese	50 mL	
¼ cup salsa	50 mL	
1 tomato, diced	1	
chopped cilantro and green onion to taste		
2, 10" (25 cm) flour tortillas, warmed	2	

1. Whisk eggs with water, salt and pepper in a medium bowl.
2. Spray a medium skillet with cooking spray. Preheat to medium.
3. Pour egg mixture into skillet. As mixture sets at the edges, with spatula, gently lift cooked portion to allow uncooked egg to flow underneath. Cook until bottom is set and top is almost set.
4. Spoon beans along the centre of the omelette. Top with cheese and salsa.
5. Fold sides of omelette over filling.
6. Cut omelette in half and transfer to warm plates. Top each serving with tomato, cilantro and onion.
7. Serve with tortillas.

Makes 2 servings
Preparation: 9 minutes
Cooking: 6 minutes

Nutrients per serving
Calories: 434   Protein: 23.4 g
Carbohydrate: 42.0 g   Fat: 18.9 g

Cathy Fowler
Brandon, Manitoba

* Refried beans (*frijoles refritos*) are mashed, cooked pinto (red Mexican) beans. Mashed black or kidney beans may also be used. The mashed beans are sautéed in butter or vegetable oil and often seasoned with minced onion, garlic, thyme, hot pepper flakes, chili powder and salt. Chopped fresh tomato and lime juice are optional. Canned refried beans are available in most supermarkets.

tomato & pesto omelette

This is simple and delicious. Parmesan cheese is also excellent with this omelette.

2 eggs	2
1 tbsp pesto sauce	15 mL
4-5 sun-dried tomatoes in oil, chopped	4-5
grated Emmenthal cheese* to taste	
½ tomato, sliced	½
walnuts, sunflower OR sesame seeds to taste	

Makes 1 serving
Preparation: 4 minutes
Cooking: 6 minutes

1 Whisk eggs with pesto and sun-dried tomatoes in a small bowl.

2 Spray a small non-stick skillet with cooking spray. Preheat to medium.

3 Pour egg mixture into skillet. As mixture sets at the edges, with spatula, gently lift cooked portion to allow uncooked egg to flow underneath. Cook until bottom is set and top is almost set, about 5 minutes.

4 Sprinkle Emmenthal cheese on half of the omelette. Place tomato slices on the cheese. Sprinkle with chopped walnuts, sunflower seeds or sesame seeds. Fold gently in half.

5 Serve omelette on a warm plate.

Nutrients per serving
Calories: 245   Protein: 14.8 g
Carbohydrate: 6.9 g   Fat: 17.9 g

Nathalie Geneviève Drolet
Ste-Foy, Quebec

* Emmenthal is the classic Swiss cheese. Named for Switzerland's Emmental Valley, it has a buttery, nutty flavour and its appearance is characterized by marble-sized holes. France, Germany and Canada also make very good Emmenthal cheeses.

mediterranean frittata

*The sun-drenched flavours of capers, artichokes, tomatoes and feta cheese
are a classic combination.*

3 eggs	3
2 tbsp crumbled feta cheese	30 mL
1 tbsp sun-dried tomatoes in oil, slivered	15 mL
1 tsp capers	5 mL
2 marinated artichoke hearts *, chopped	2
freshly ground pepper to taste	

1 Beat eggs in a medium bowl. Stir in remaining ingredients.

2 Spray a non-stick medium skillet with cooking spray. Heat until hot.

3 Pour egg mixture into skillet. Cover and cook over medium heat until eggs are set, 5 to 6 minutes.

4 Sprinkle lightly with pepper. Slide onto a warm plate.

5 Cut the frittata in wedges and serve.

Makes 1 to 2 servings
Preparation: 5 minutes
Cooking: 6 minutes

Nutrients per serving
Calories: 365   Protein: 23.8 g
Carbohydrate: 11.7 g Fat: 25.2 g

Robin Hushagen
Calgary, Alberta

* The globe artichoke is the type of artichoke most familiar to Canadians. Used in appetizers, salads, etc., it is the bud of a thistle-related plant. Bottled, marinated artichokes are available in most supermarkets. Artichokes are also available fresh, frozen and canned.

Jerusalem and Chinese/Japanese artichokes are unrelated plants.

prosciutto, asiago & asparagus omelette

Asparagus and prosciutto seem to be made for one another. They taste even better with eggs. Hot capicollo is a delicious variation if prosciutto is unavailable.

2 eggs	2	
2 tbsp water	30 mL	
pepper to taste		
1 tbsp butter	15 mL	
2 thin slices prosciutto, cut into strips	2	
3 asparagus stalks*, cooked, cut in bite-sized lengths	3	
1/4 cup grated Asiago cheese	50 mL	

Makes 1 serving
Preparation: 6 minutes
Cooking: 6 minutes

1 Whisk eggs with water and pepper in a small bowl.

2 Melt butter in an 8" (20 cm) non-stick skillet over medium-high heat.

3 Pour eggs into skillet; gently push set eggs at the edge toward the middle so uncooked eggs reach hot skillet surface. Cook until eggs are almost set, about 4 minutes.

4 Place prosciutto on half of the omelette while the eggs are still moist. Arrange asparagus on prosciutto. Sprinkle cheese over asparagus.

5 Fold omelette over filling. Serve on a warm plate.

Nutrients per serving
Calories: 385   Protein: 22.0 g
Carbohydrate: 4.2 g   Fat: 31.1 g

Kim Robshaw
Windsor, Ontario

* A member of the lily family, asparagus (sparrow grass) was cultivated by the ancient Romans. In Belgium, France and Germany, white asparagus is preferred; in England, Italy and North America the preference is for coloured asparagus, ranging from pale to dark green with purple tips. Choose firm stalks with tight tips and wash well as asparagus is grown in sandy soil.

spicy pepper & onion frittata

Congo peppers, native to Trinidad, are extremely hot.
How much you use depends on how hot you like your food.

4 eggs	4	1	Whisk eggs in a medium bowl and set aside.
1 large Congo pepper* OR 2 jalapeños	1	2	Remove seeds from hot pepper. Chop pepper finely and set aside.
1 tsp olive oil	5 mL	3	Heat oil in a small non-stick skillet.
1 small onion, diced	1	4	Sauté onion until soft but not brown. Stir in mustard, then hot peppers.
½ tsp mustard	2 mL		

5 Pour eggs into skillet. As eggs set at the edges, with spatula, gently lift cooked portion and tilt skillet to allow uncooked egg to flow underneath. Cook until bottom is set and top is almost set.

Makes 2 servings
Preparation: 6 minutes
Cooking: 12 minutes

6 Flip the frittata and cook briefly on the second side**.

Nutrients per serving
Calories: 183   Protein: 13.0 g
Carbohydrate: 4.6 g   Fat: 12.2 g

Helen Lee
Markham, Ontario

* The habañero pepper family (*Capsicum chinense*) includes many varieties. They are known as Congo peppers in Trinidad, bonney peppers in Barbados and Scotch bonnets in Jamaica. They are the hottest peppers in the world, 50 to 100 times hotter than jalapeños. About 1 to 1½" (2.5 to 5 cm) in size, one Trinidad variety is called Seven Pots as one pepper can flavour 7 pots of food. Hot peppers (chilies or chiles) are related to tomatoes, potatoes, eggplant and tobacco.

** If you prefer, use an ovenproof skillet and place under a preheated broiler for a few seconds to set frittata top.

note

Be sure to scrub hands and nails carefully after handling hot chilies. The volatile oils found in them can irritate your skin. If you have sensitive skin, it is best to wear rubber gloves when handling hot peppers.

taco tortilla omelette

A tasty way to use up leftover taco filling, these are messy but kids love them and they are filling. Freeze taco meat in plastic containers and defrost as needed.

4 eggs	4
¼ cup milk	50 mL
salt and pepper to taste	
1 cup taco meat mixture	250 mL
1 tbsp butter	15 mL
1 green onion, chopped	1
½ cup shredded Tex Mex cheese	125 mL
6, 10" (25 cm) flour tortillas, warmed	6
chopped tomato for topping	
sour cream for topping	
salsa for topping	

1. Whisk eggs, milk, salt and pepper together in a small bowl. Set aside.

2. Heat taco meat in a saucepan or in a microwave until hot. Keep warm.

3. Melt butter in a large non-stick skillet. Sauté green onion over medium heat until soft.

4. Pour eggs into hot skillet with onion. As mixture sets at the edges, with spatula, gently lift cooked portion to allow uncooked egg to flow underneath. Cook over medium-low heat until just firm, about 10 minutes. Spoon warm taco meat and shredded cheese over omelette. Cover skillet until cheese melts.

5. Place 1 warm tortilla on each of 6 dinner plates. Top each with a healthy slice of taco omelette.

6. Top with tomato, sour cream and salsa, as desired. Roll up tortillas and enjoy.

Makes 6 servings
Preparation: 6 minutes
Cooking: 12 minutes

Lynn Lilje
Surrey, British Columbia

Nutrients per serving
Calories: 376   Protein: 19.2 g
Carbohydrate: 34.3 g   Fat: 17.5 g

note

When you are making tacos, be sure to make extra taco filling so that you can make these the next day. Even without tortillas this omelette is delicious.

eggsquisite olé fajita

Delicious and versatile – vary the sauce, cheese or vegetables. Try béchamel sauce and use a combination of seafood or ham, Cheddar cheese and broccoli. Everyone will love it!

1 green onion, sliced	1
4 eggs	4
4 tbsp water	60 mL
¼ tsp garlic salt	1 mL
freshly ground pepper to taste	
½ celery stalk, sliced	½
½ carrot, cut in thin strips	½
¼ green pepper, sliced	¼
4 mushrooms, sliced	4
¼ cup shredded cheese	50 mL
1 tbsp salsa	15 mL
2 strips bacon, cooked, crumbled	2

Makes 2 servings
Preparation: 13 minutes
Cooking: 17 minutes

Nutrients per serving
Calories: 305   Protein: 19.8 g
Carbohydrate: 6.5 g   Fat: 22.1 g

1   Whisk together onion, eggs, water, garlic salt and pepper.

2   Spray a medium non-stick skillet with cooking spray. Preheat to medium.

3   Pour half of egg mixture into skillet. As mixture sets at the edges, with spatula, gently lift cooked portion to allow uncooked egg to flow underneath. Cook until bottom is set and top is almost set. Slide onto a plate and keep warm. Repeat procedure to make a second omelette. Keep warm.

4   Spray skillet again and sauté celery, carrot, peppers and mushrooms until tender-crisp.

5   Spoon half of the vegetable mixture onto each omelette. Sprinkle with cheese, salsa and bacon. Fold lower edge of omelette toward the centre; fold in sides to make a fajita.

Paul Chouinard
St-Étienne-des-Grès, Quebec

arabian-style stuffed omelette

This makes a tasty dinner with a salad of mixed greens and sliced oranges.

3 tbsp oil, divided	45 mL
20 peanuts, minced	20
½ cup thinly sliced onion	125 mL
2 tsp sugar	10 mL
1½ tbsp soy sauce	22 mL
⅛ tsp black pepper	0.5 mL
½ lb cooked meat*, minced	250 g
2 garlic cloves, thinly sliced	2
6 eggs	6

Makes 2 servings
Preparation: 7 minutes
Cooking: 20 minutes

Nutrients per serving
Calories: 713   Protein: 56.4 g
Carbohydrate: 11.9 g   Fat: 48.1 g

1 Heat 1 tbsp (15 mL) oil in a small skillet. Stir in peanuts. Cook and stir on medium-low for 5 to 10 minutes, or until peanuts are lightly browned.

2 Add onion, sugar, soy sauce and pepper; cook for 2 minutes. Stir in meat. Set aside and keep warm.

3 Heat 1 tbsp (15 mL) oil and half of the garlic in a large non-stick skillet. When garlic softens, pour in 3 beaten eggs.

4 As eggs set at the edges, with spatula, gently lift cooked portion to allow uncooked egg to flow underneath. Cook until bottom is set and top is almost set. Slide omelette onto a warm plate.

5 Repeat to make a second omelette.

6 Fill each omelette with half of the meat mixture. Fold and serve.

Azim Khot
Thornhill, Ontario

* Try cooked beef, chicken or pork.

sushi omelette

Pickled ginger and wasabi add zesty fire to this fresh and colourful omelette.

2 eggs	**2**
1 tbsp soy sauce	**15 mL**
¼ cup julienned cucumber	**50 mL**
½ cup crabmeat OR **imitation crab**	**125 mL**
¼ cup diced avocado	**50 mL**
handful of chopped watercress *	

Makes 1 serving
Preparation: 8 minutes
Cooking: 4 minutes

Nutrients per serving
Calories: 268   Protein: 24.4 g
Carbohydrate: 6.1 g   Fat: 16.2 g

1. Whisk eggs and soy sauce together in a small bowl.

2. Spray a medium non-stick skillet lightly with cooking spray. Heat over medium-high heat until hot.

3. Pour egg mixture into skillet, swirling to coat skillet with eggs. Lift edges of omelette during cooking to allow uncooked egg to flow underneath. Cook until eggs are just set.

4. Place cucumber, crab, avocado and watercress on half of the omelette.

5. Fold the omelette and slide carefully onto a warm plate.

Gillian da Silva
Oshawa, Ontario

* Watercress is part of the mustard family. Its peppery flavour is delicious in sandwiches, soups and salads. Store watercress for up to a week in the refrigerator with the stems in a glass of water and the leaves loosely covered with a plastic bag.

oriental omelette

*A terrific dinner omelette, you can skip the baking if you're really hungry,
but this is lovely when it comes out of the oven.*

¼ cup chicken broth	50 mL
¼ cup EACH diced green pepper, onion and sliced water chestnuts	50 mL
1 cup cooked rice	250 mL
½ cup chopped cooked chicken	125 mL
2 tbsp low-sodium soy sauce	30 mL
4 eggs	4
¼ - ½ cup milk	50 - 125 mL
2 tbsp hoisin sauce	30 mL

1 Heat chicken broth in a medium non-stick skillet. Add green pepper, onion and water chestnuts; cook vegetables until tender, about 5 minutes.

2 Transfer vegetables to a medium bowl; stir in rice, chicken and soy sauce. Set aside.

3 Whisk eggs and milk in a small bowl.

4 Spray the same skillet with cooking spray. Heat until hot.

5 Pour egg mixture into hot skillet. As mixture sets at the edges, with spatula, gently lift cooked portion to allow uncooked egg to flow underneath. Cook until bottom is set and top is almost set, about 3 minutes. Carefully flip and cook 3 more minutes.

6 Transfer omelette to a 12" (30 cm) baking dish. Spoon rice mixture over half of omelette. Fold other half over filling.

7 Cover dish with foil. Bake at 350°F (180°C) for 20 minutes.

8 Drizzle hoisin sauce over omelette before serving.

Makes 2 servings
Preparation: 12 minutes
Cooking: 30 minutes

Kathy King MacLean
Bedford, Nova Scotia

Nutrients per serving
Calories: 438   Protein: 29.0 g
Carbohydrate: 46.4 g   Fat: 14.2 g

dijon, pecan & asparagus omelette,
page 78

vegetarian

water chestnut surprise

Crunchy texture and great flavour make this simple omelette a very pleasant surprise.

2 eggs	2	
¼ cup slivered water chestnuts	50 mL	
2 tbsp finely diced old Cheddar cheese	30 mL	
1 tbsp EACH chopped onion and green pepper	15 mL	

Makes 1 serving
Preparation: 6 minutes
Cooking: 7 minutes

1 Whisk eggs in a medium bowl.

2 Stir in remaining ingredients.

3 Spray a small non-stick skillet with cooking spray. Preheat to medium.

4 Pour egg mixture into skillet. As mixture sets at the edges, with spatula, lift cooked portion to allow uncooked egg to flow underneath. Cook until bottom and top are set.

5 Fold omelette in half when fully cooked. Serve on a warm plate.

Nutrients per serving
Calories: 248　　Protein: 17.2 g
Carbohydrate: 9.8 g　　Fat: 15.4 g

Lindsay Lamarche
North Bay, Ontario

two-cheese frittata

This frittata is enough for four when served with a salad and multi-grain bread.

5 eggs	5
½ tsp salt	2 mL
¼ tsp baking powder	1 mL
½ tsp grapeseed oil	2 mL
1 cup cottage cheese	250 mL
¼ lb aged Cheddar cheese, sliced	125 g

Makes 3 to 4 servings
Preparation: 6 minutes
Cooking: 14 minutes

1 Whisk eggs with salt and baking powder in a medium bowl.

2 Heat oil in a medium non-stick skillet.

3 Pour eggs into skillet. Spoon cottage cheese over the eggs.

4 Cover the frittata with thin slices of Cheddar cheese.

5 Cover the skillet and cook over medium-low heat until cooked through.

6 Cut into wedges to serve.

Nutrients per serving
Calories: 261　　Protein: 22.5 g
Carbohydrate: 2.9 g　　Fat: 17.2 g

Susan Karamessines
Duncan, British Columbia

basil omelette

Fresh and delicious, this omelette is sure to be a favourite throughout the summer when basil is at its peak. Also try this with lemon basil.

4 eggs	**4**	
salt and pepper to taste		
1 tbsp olive oil	**15 mL**	
¼ cup finely chopped fresh basil* leaves	**50 mL**	
¼ cup shredded Swiss cheese	**50 mL**	

1. Whisk eggs, salt and pepper in a small bowl.

2. Heat oil in a medium non-stick skillet. Add basil; cook over medium-low heat until fragrant and bubbly, 1 to 2 minutes.

3. Pour eggs into skillet. As eggs set at the edges, with spatula, gently lift cooked portion to allow uncooked egg to flow underneath. Cook until bottom is set and top is almost set.

4. Sprinkle cheese over the omelette. Continue cooking until the cheese melts.

5. Serve this omelette with chopped or sliced tomatoes drizzled with olive oil.

Makes 2 servings
Preparation: 6 minutes
Cooking: 9 minutes

Nutrients per serving
Calories: 259   Protein: 16.5 g
Carbohydrate: 1.3 g   Fat: 20.6 g

France Drouin
Ste-Foy, Quebec

* Basil is an important ingredient in Mediterranean recipes. Ancient Greeks called it the royal herb (*basilikos* royal). A member of the mint family, basil is very aromatic, with a licorice/clove/mint flavour. Lemon, cinnamon, clove and anise basils are available, as well as a Blue African and purple-leafed opal basil. Store basil, refrigerated, with the stems in a glass of water and cover loosely with a plastic bag. Fresh basil is also known as an effective mosquito or bug repellent.

olive & red pepper frittata

The rich pungent flavours of green and black olives highlight this frittata.
It could also be cut into smaller wedges and served as an appetizer.

8 eggs	8	
1 green onion, chopped	1	
¼ cup chopped green olives*	50 mL	
¼ cup chopped black olives*	50 mL	
1 small red pepper, chopped	1	
salt and pepper to taste		
1 cup shredded Cheddar cheese	250 mL	

Makes 4 servings
Preparation: 10 minutes
Cooking: 15 minutes

1 Whisk eggs in a medium bowl with onion, olives, red pepper, salt and pepper.

2 Spray a large non-stick skillet with cooking spray. Preheat to medium.

3 Pour egg mixture into the skillet. Cook over medium-low heat until eggs are set, about 15 minutes. If you prefer, cover the skillet so the eggs set more quickly.

4 Sprinkle the cheese over the frittata.

5 Cut the frittata into wedges and serve as soon as the cheese melts.

Nutrients per serving
Calories: 284   Protein: 19.8 g
Carbohydrate: 3.0 g   Fat: 21.3 g

Richelle Necker
Calgary, Alberta

* Olive trees are native to Mediterranean countries and were considered sacred as long ago as 1700 B.C. Ripe olives come in both green and black versions. Kalamata olives from Greece are almond-shaped with a rich, sweet flavour and a dark eggplant colour. Niçoise olives from France are oval and dark brown, with a mellow, nutty flavour. Spiced olives, both green and black, are seasoned with herbs and dried chili peppers. They add extra zest to any recipe.

"scarborough fair" fresh herb omelette

This omelette is delicious and versatile. Use fresh herbs when possible – if fresh herbs aren't available, substitute with one-third the amount of dried herbs.

4 eggs	4
1 tsp EACH chopped fresh parsley, rosemary*, thyme and oregano	5 mL
salt and pepper to taste	
2 tbsp grated Parmesan cheese	30 mL

Makes 2 servings
Preparation: 6 minutes
Cooking: 8 minutes

Nutrients per serving
Calories: 175   Protein: 15.0 g
Carbohydrate: 1.1 g   Fat: 11.8 g

1 Whisk eggs in a medium bowl. Stir in minced herbs, salt and pepper.

2 Spray a medium non-stick skillet with cooking spray. Preheat to medium.

3 Pour egg mixture into skillet. As mixture sets at the edges, with spatula, gently lift cooked portion to allow uncooked egg to flow underneath. Cook until bottom is set and top is almost set.

4 Sprinkle Parmesan cheese over half of the omelette. Fold gently.

5 Cut the omelette in half and transfer to 2 warm plates.

Jim Pound
St. Catharines, Ontario

* Aromatic rosemary grows wild on hillsides throughout much of the Mediterranean area. A member of the mint family, it has been used for over 2,500 years to flavour soups, salads and egg and meat dishes. The lemony pine flavour is pungent, so use rosemary sparingly.

Rosemary is also used in perfumes, cosmetics and aromatherapy, where it is reputed to enhance mental clarity and relax the nerves.

dijon, pecan & asparagus omelette

This omelette is very "well-stuffed" with an elegant combination of flavours.

2½ tbsp butter, divided	37 mL
½ cup pecan pieces	125 mL
1 tbsp Dijon mustard	15 mL
10 asparagus spears, cut into bite-sized pieces	10
4 eggs	4
4 tsp water	20 mL
salt and pepper to taste	
2 tbsp light sour cream	30 mL

1. Melt 1½ tbsp (22 mL) of butter in a medium saucepan over medium heat. Add pecans; toss and sauté 2 minutes.

2. Stir in mustard. Add asparagus; sauté for another 5 minutes on medium-low. Keep warm.

3. Beat 2 eggs and 2 tsp (10 mL) water in a small bowl. Sprinkle with salt and pepper.

4. Melt ½ tbsp (7 mL) butter in a medium skillet. Pour in eggs. As eggs set at the edges, with spatula, gently lift cooked portion to allow uncooked egg to flow underneath. Cook until bottom is set and top is almost set.

5. Spoon half of the filling over half of the omelette. Drizzle 1 tbsp (15 mL) sour cream over filling before folding.

6. Repeat the process to make a second omelette.

Makes 2 servings
Preparation: 4 minutes
Cooking: 15 minutes

Nutrients per serving
Calories: 491   Protein: 17.9 g
Carbohydrate: 11.6 g   Fat: 43.2 g

Lisa Harrison
Vancouver, British Columbia

spicy spinach & pepper frittata

*Very substantial, this colourful frittata can be varied to suit
your preferred "heat" level – adjust to taste.*

2 tbsp butter, divided	30 mL
1 onion, finely chopped	1
1 garlic clove, minced	1
1 small hot pepper, sliced	1
10 oz bag spinach, trimmed	284 g
1 EACH red, orange and green peppers, finely chopped	1
¼ tsp EACH salt, pepper, paprika, curry powder and garlic powder, or more, to taste	1 mL
6 eggs	6
2 tbsp water	30 mL
4-6 tbsp cream cheese	60-90 mL

1 Melt 1 tbsp (15 mL) of butter in a large non-stick skillet over medium-high heat. Add onion and garlic; cook for 2 minutes, stirring often.

2 Stir in hot pepper, spinach, peppers and half the spices; cover and cook for 4 minutes, stirring once, or just until spinach wilts.

3 Whisk eggs, water and remaining spices in a medium bowl. Stir in spinach mixture.

4 Melt 1 tbsp (15 mL) butter in the same skillet over medium heat. Pour in egg mixture. Cook, stirring gently, for about 30 seconds.

5 Spoon dollops of cream cheese over frittata. Gently lift cooked portion, with spatula, to allow uncooked egg to flow underneath.

6 Cook, without stirring, for about 2 minutes longer, or until top is almost set and bottom is golden.

7 Slide the frittata onto a large plate. Invert skillet over plate; invert again to return frittata to skillet.*

8 Cook for 1 to 2 minutes, or until a knife inserted into the centre comes out clean.

9 Cut into wedges and serve on warm plates.

Makes 2 generous servings
Preparation: 15 minutes
Cooking: 18 minutes

Nutrients per serving
Calories: 528   Protein: 27.5 g
Carbohydrate: 24.6 g Fat: 37.4 g

Lincoln McCardle
Toronto, Ontario

* If you prefer, use an ovenproof skillet and place under a preheated broiler for a few seconds to set frittata top.

spinach frittata

Crushed coriander and mustard seeds give this frittata a very pleasant, subtle crunch.

2 tbsp butter, divided	30 mL
1 medium onion, finely chopped	1
1 tbsp minced fresh ginger	15 mL
1 tsp crushed coriander seeds	5 mL
1 tsp black mustard seeds	5 mL
10 oz bag spinach, trimmed	284 g
1/4 tsp salt, divided	1 mL
6 eggs	6
2 tbsp water	30 mL
1/4 tsp pepper	1 mL

Makes 4 servings
Preparation: 10 minutes
Cooking: 10 minutes

Nutrients per serving
Calories: 192   Protein: 11.8 g
Carbohydrate: 6.3 g   Fat: 13.7 g

1   Melt 1 tbsp (15 mL) butter in a large non-stick skillet over medium-high heat. Cook onion, ginger, coriander and mustard seeds for 2 minutes, stirring constantly.

2   Add spinach and half of the salt. Cover and cook for 4 minutes, or until spinach wilts, stirring once halfway through.

3   Whisk eggs, water, pepper and remaining salt in a medium bowl. Stir in spinach mixture.

4   Melt 1 tbsp (15 mL) butter in same skillet over medium heat. Pour in egg mixture. Cook, stirring gently, for about 30 seconds, lifting edges with spatula to allow uncooked egg to flow underneath.

5   Cook, without stirring, for about 2 minutes longer, or until top is almost set and bottom is golden.

6   Slide the frittata onto a large plate. Invert skillet over plate; invert again to return frittata to skillet*.

7   Cook for 1 to 2 minutes, or until knife inserted into centre comes out clean.

8   Cut into wedges and serve on warm plates.

Debora Miscione
Dundas, Ontario

* If you prefer, use an ovenproof skillet and place under a preheated broiler for a few seconds to set frittata top.

tomato ginger omelette

The fresh tomato ginger salsa is zesty and colourful, a terrific complement to this omelette.

tomato ginger salsa

1 large ripe tomato, seeded, diced	1
¼ cup EACH chopped red and green peppers	50 mL
1 tsp olive oil	5 mL
½ tsp finely grated fresh ginger	2 mL
½ tsp rice wine vinegar	2 mL
salt and pepper to taste	
2 eggs	2
salt and pepper to taste	

Makes 1 serving
Preparation: 7 minutes
Cooking: 5 minutes

1 Combine the tomato, peppers, olive oil, ginger and vinegar in a medium bowl to make the salsa. Season with salt and pepper. Set aside.

2 Break eggs into a small bowl. Beat with a fork until foamy. Add salt and pepper.

3 Spray a non-stick skillet with cooking spray. Preheat to medium.

4 Pour eggs into skillet. As eggs set at the edges, with spatula, gently lift cooked portion to allow uncooked egg to flow underneath. Cook until bottom is set and top is almost set.

5 Spoon half of the salsa onto half of the omelette. Fold other half of the omelette over salsa.

6 Garnish omelette with more salsa at serving time.

Charles Long
Gatineau, Quebec

Nutrients per serving
Calories: 242   Protein: 14.4 g
Carbohydrate: 13.6 g   Fat: 15.1 g

eggplant & tomato omelette

Let the eggplant brown nicely – it will add to the flavour of this tasty omelette.

1 tbsp olive oil	15 mL	1
1 cup chopped eggplant *	250 mL	
½ cup chopped tomato	125 mL	
1 small onion, chopped	1	
salt and pepper to taste		
3 eggs	3	

1. Heat oil in a medium skillet. Add eggplant, tomato and onion. Sauté on medium-high, stirring often, until all vegetables are tender and eggplant is nicely browned, 6 to 7 minutes. Sprinkle with salt and pepper. Set aside and keep warm.

2. Whisk eggs in a small bowl.

3. Spray a small non-stick skillet with cooking spray. Preheat to medium. Pour eggs into skillet. Cook until egg is almost set, lifting edges to let uncooked egg flow underneath.

4. Flip omelette to brown other side.

5. Slide omelette onto a plate. Spoon vegetables on half. Fold gently.

Makes 1 serving
Preparation: 7 minutes
Cooking: 10 minutes

Nutrients per serving
Calories: 282   Protein: 20.7 g
Carbohydrate: 15.9 g   Fat: 15.3 g

Amber Phillips
Squamish, British Columbia

* Young eggplants (aubergines) do not need to be peeled. Look for smaller, baby Italian eggplants, or the slender oriental/Japanese eggplants, for the most delicate flavour.

Related to tomatoes and potatoes, the versatile eggplant may be baked, grilled, sautéed, boiled or puréed. It is seasoned with garlic and thyme in France; with dill, garlic, lemon and yogurt in Turkey; with garlic, tahini and tomatoes in Greece; with various curry blends in India. Caponata, Parmigiana, Ratatouille, Eggplant Provençal, Baba Ghanouj and Moussaka are just a few popular eggplant dishes.

eggplant omelette

For the best flavour, be sure to use good quality Parmesan cheese – it's worth the extra cost.

2 tbsp butter, divided	30 mL	
1 cup diced eggplant	250 mL	
1/3 cup Parmesan cheese	75 mL	
1/2 tsp chopped chervil *	2 mL	
6 eggs	6	
1/4 cup milk	50 mL	
1/2 garlic clove, minced	1/2	
1 shallot, minced	1	
salt and pepper to taste		

1 Melt 1 tbsp (15 mL) butter in a medium non-stick skillet. Heat until skillet is hot and butter bubbles.

2 Sauté eggplant in butter for 4 to 6 minutes, or until browned.

3 Remove eggplant from skillet; sprinkle with Parmesan cheese and chervil; set aside.

4 Beat eggs, milk, garlic, shallot, salt and pepper in a medium bowl.

5 Melt 1 tbsp (15 mL) butter in the same skillet over medium heat.

6 Pour egg mixture into skillet. As mixture sets at the edges, with spatula, gently lift cooked portion to allow uncooked egg to flow underneath. Cook until bottom is set and top is almost set.

7 Spoon the eggplant filling over half of the omelette. Fold gently.

8 Slide the omelette onto a warm serving plate. Cut into 4 wedges.

Makes 4 servings
Preparation: 6 minutes
Cooking: 12 minutes

Nutrients per serving
Calories: 213   Protein: 13.5 g
Carbohydrate: 3.3 g   Fat: 16.0 g

Guy Gosselin
St-Nicéphore, Quebec

* Chervil has a subtle anise aroma and mild parsley-like flavour. The delicate leaves resemble carrot tops. Chervil is used by French cooks as part of a *fines herbes* mixture and in *bouquet garni*.

Also called *cicily* and *sweet cicily*, it is frequently used in egg dishes, and with mild cheese, chicken and fish.

fresh green bean omelette

A light, fresh-tasting omelette, make this when the green beans in your garden are perfect. Serve it with salsa – choose the heat level that suits your taste buds.

5 long, thin green beans	5
2-3 tbsp water	30-45 mL
1 tsp olive oil	5 mL
1 green onion, chopped	1
2 eggs	2
salt and pepper to taste	
salsa OR chopped tomato to taste	

Makes 1 serving
Preparation: 3 minutes
Cooking: 7 minutes

Nutrients per serving
Calories: 195   Protein: 12.9 g
Carbohydrate: 2.9 g   Fat: 14.4 g

1   Wash and trim green beans. Heat water in a small skillet. When water boils, add beans; cover and cook for 2 minutes. Drain beans and set aside.

2   Heat oil in the same skillet. Add onion and cook over medium heat until onion softens.

3   Whisk eggs with salt and pepper.

4   Pour eggs into skillet over onion. Cook gently. As eggs set at the edges, with spatula, lift cooked portion to allow uncooked egg to flow underneath. Cook until egg is set and bottom has just begun to brown.

5   Place beans on half of the omelette. Fold other half over beans.

6   Serve with salsa or chopped tomato, as desired.

Barb Rudyk
Vermilion, Alberta

variation

Substitute asparagus for green beans when asparagus is in season.

jalapeño jack, artichoke & mushroom omelette

Adding whole-grain bread or rolls and a marinated vegetable or fruit salad to round out the meal would stretch this omelette to two servings.

¼ tsp butter	1 mL	
¼ cup sliced fresh mushrooms	50 mL	
¼ cup grated Jalapeño Monterey Jack cheese*	50 mL	
2 small canned artichokes, finely chopped	2	
3 eggs	3	
1 tsp butter (optional)	5 mL	

Makes 1 to 2 servings
Preparation: 7 minutes
Cooking: 5 minutes

Nutrients per serving
Calories: 379   Protein: 28.7 g
Carbohydrate: 11.5 g Fat: 24.6 g

* Jalapeño Monterey Jack cheese is available in the deli section of many supermarkets. If you cannot find it, add minced fresh or bottled jalapeño peppers, to taste, to shredded Monterey Jack cheese.

Mild, soft-textured Jack cheese is named after David Jacks, who created it in California in the 1800s. Unaged Jack cheese melts well and is very good in omelettes or sandwiches. Aged Jack cheese has a deeper colour, nuttier flavour, and may be grated for use in omelettes or salads.

1 Melt butter in a medium non-stick skillet over medium heat. Add mushrooms and sauté until softened. Transfer to a medium bowl.

2 Stir cheese and artichokes into mushrooms. Set aside.

3 Whisk eggs in a small bowl.

4 Spray the same skillet with cooking spray and preheat to medium, or melt butter if you prefer.

5 Pour eggs into skillet, rotating to evenly distribute the eggs. Cook for 30 to 50 seconds, or until eggs are still slightly damp and shiny.

6 Spread mushroom mixture quickly over half of the omelette. Fold the other half over filling.

7 Slide the omelette onto a warm plate and serve.

Linda Anselmo
Surrey, British Columbia

curried potato & green chile omelette

This omelette is superb – very satisfying, with full-bodied flavour.
Use the curry paste that suits your preference.

½ tbsp olive OR vegetable oil	7 mL	
2 tbsp chopped onion	30 mL	
1 tbsp finely chopped jalapeño OR mild green chili pepper	15 mL	
¼ cup chopped zucchini	50 mL	
½ cup chopped, cooked potato	125 mL	
½ tbsp mild to hot curry paste*	7 mL	
salt to taste		
2 eggs	2	
1 tbsp water	15 mL	

Makes 1 generous serving
Preparation: 10 minutes
Cooking: 10 minutes

1 Heat oil in a medium non-stick skillet. Sauté onion until softened.

2 Stir in peppers, zucchini and potato. Cook and stir until zucchini is tender. Stir in curry paste and salt. Remove from skillet and keep warm.

3 Beat eggs and water until foamy.

4 Spray the same skillet with cooking spray. Preheat to medium.

5 Pour eggs into skillet. As eggs set at the edges, with spatula, lift cooked portion to allow uncooked egg to flow underneath. Cook until bottom is set and top is almost set.

6 Spread potato filling over half of the omelette. Fold other half over filling.

7 Cover skillet; let stand 2 to 3 minutes over low heat until omelette is puffed.

8 Slide the omelette onto a warm plate. Serve with mango chutney and toasted French bread.

Julie Davidson
Halifax, Nova Scotia

Nutrients per serving
Calories: 323   Protein: 14.5 g
Carbohydrate: 21.0 g   Fat: 20.3 g

* For a hot curry paste, to balance the mild flavour of the potatoes, try vindaloo curry paste, a very flavourful blend of mustard and cumin seeds, ginger, garlic, red chilies, wine vinegar, black pepper, tamarind and more. A specialty of Goa and central and southwestern India, the name *vindaloo* is of Portuguese origin. It means wine and garlic.

note

To quickly cook the potato, pierce a scrubbed potato several times with a sharp knife and microwave on HIGH (100%) for 3 to 4 minutes, or until tender.

vegetable *frittata*

The sautéed carrot gives this frittata a delicate sweetness.

1 tbsp vegetable oil	15 mL
1 cup bite-sized broccoli florets	250 mL
½ cup shredded carrot	125 mL
½ cup chopped onion	125 mL
½ cup chopped red pepper	125 mL
4 eggs	4
¼ cup milk	50 mL
1 tbsp chopped parsley	15 mL
¼ tsp salt	1 mL
¼ tsp hot pepper sauce	1 mL
¾ cup grated Cheddar cheese	175 mL
1 tbsp grated Parmesan cheese	15 mL

1 Heat the oil in a medium non-stick skillet.

2 Add broccoli, carrot, and onion. Cook over medium heat for 5 minutes, or until broccoli is tender-crisp.

3 Stir in red peppers; cook for 1 minute.

4 Whisk eggs with milk, parsley, salt and hot pepper sauce until blended. Pour into skillet over vegetables. Turn heat to low.

5 Sprinkle the cheeses over the frittata. Cover and cook for 5 to 10 minutes, or until eggs are set.

6 Cut into wedges and serve.

Makes 2 to 3 servings
Preparation: 11 minutes
Cooking: 13 minutes

Ethel St. Jean
New Liskeard, Ontario

Nutrients per serving
Calories: 224   Protein: 13.5 g
Carbohydrate: 6.3 g   Fat: 16.3 g

leftover feast omelette

This omelette is very substantial, with delicious flavours. The brown rice adds great texture. Cut and serve the omelette right from the skillet.

1 cup diced onion	250 mL
1½ cups diced red, yellow OR green peppers	375 mL
4 eggs	4
8 egg whites	8
minced fresh basil to taste	
1 cup cooked brown rice*	250 mL
1 cup shredded Cheddar cheese	250 mL
4 tbsp ranch salad dressing	60 mL

Makes 4 servings
Preparation: 12 minutes
Cooking: 15 minutes

1. Spray a large non-stick skillet with cooking spray.
2. Cook onion and peppers over medium-high heat until slightly browned, about 5 minutes.
3. Whisk eggs and whites together in a medium bowl.
4. Pour eggs into skillet over onion and peppers. Sprinkle basil over eggs. Cook over medium heat. As mixture sets at the edges, with spatula, gently lift cooked portion to allow uncooked egg to flow underneath. Cook until bottom is set and top is almost set.
5. Spread rice and cheese over half of the omelette. Fold other half over filling. Continue cooking until eggs are fully cooked.
6. Divide into 4 portions. Drizzle 1 tbsp (15 mL) ranch dressing over each serving.

Tiana DiMichele
Scarborough, Ontario

Nutrients per serving
Calories: 372   Protein: 22.4 g
Carbohydrate: 20.1 g   Fat: 22.5 g

* Brown rice retains the high-fibre, nutritious bran coating. However, the bran also makes brown rice subject to becoming rancid – it can only be stored for about 6 months. The flavour is nutty and the texture is slightly chewy. Cooking time is about 30 minutes.

note

Save leftover egg yolks to use in savoury sauces such as Hollandaise or Mayonnaise, or in luscious desserts such as Lemon Curd (Lemon Butter), Lemon Pie Filling, Crème Caramel or Crème Brûlée, Zabaglione (Sabayon).

eggstravaganza omelette

Sautéed vegetables plus a tasty mushroom sauce, this hearty omelette needs only a green salad to round out a meal for two.

1 small onion, chopped	1
1 cup sliced mushrooms	250 mL
1 garlic clove, chopped	1
½ red pepper, chopped	½
5 oz* cream of mushroom soup	142 g
salt to taste	
onion and garlic pepper to taste	
4 eggs	4
4 tbsp milk	60 mL
1 cup grated marble cheese	250 mL

Makes 2 servings
Preparation: 10 minutes
Cooking: 8 minutes

1 Spray a medium non-stick skillet with cooking spray. Sauté onion, mushrooms, garlic and peppers over medium-high heat until liquid evaporates, about 3 minutes.

2 Stir in soup and seasonings; stir until heated through. Remove from skillet; keep warm.

3 Beat 2 eggs with 2 tbsp (30 mL) milk.

4 Spray the same skillet with cooking spray. Heat over medium-high heat.

5 Pour eggs into skillet. As eggs set at the edges, with spatula, gently lift cooked portion to allow uncooked egg to flow underneath. Cook until omelette is almost set, about 3 to 5 minutes.

6 Flip whole omelette over when cooked. Add half of the veggie mixture to half of the omelette. Sprinkle with half of the cheese. Fold and transfer to a warm plate.

7 Repeat the process to make a second omelette.

Deborah Martelle
Ailsa Craig, Ontario

Nutrients per serving
Calories: 491   Protein: 29.9 g
Carbohydrate: 14.6 g   Fat: 34.7 g

* This amount is half of a 10 oz (284 g) can.

note

To save time, make one omelette and cut it in half to serve. If you want to save calories, omit the soup and use ¾ cup (175 mL) of cheese.

royal fundy digby scallop omelette, page 94

meat & seafood

royal fundy digby scallop omelette

A dinner fit for royalty, indulge yourself with this succulent omelette,
or make more omelettes to treat special guests.

1 tbsp butter	15 mL
¼ lb scallops,* sliced	125 g
2-3 large mushrooms, sliced	2-3
2 tbsp EACH chopped red and green peppers	30 mL
2 tbsp chopped green onion	30 mL
2 eggs	2
2 tbsp milk	30 mL
¼ cup grated Parmesan OR Swiss cheese	50 mL

Makes 1 serving
Preparation: 10 minutes
Cooking: 8 minutes

1 Melt butter in a medium non-stick skillet. Sauté scallops lightly. Add mushrooms, peppers and onion; cook 1 minute longer. Transfer scallops and vegetables to a bowl; keep warm.

2 Whisk eggs and milk together.

3 Add a bit more butter to the same skillet, if needed. Preheat to medium.

4 Pour eggs into skillet. As eggs set at the edges, with spatula, gently lift cooked portion to allow uncooked egg to flow underneath. Cook until bottom is set and top is almost set. Sprinkle with cheese. Continue cooking until eggs are set.

5 Spoon scallop mixture over half of the omelette. Fold in half and serve.

Angela O'Neil
Digby, Nova Scotia

Nutrients per serving
Calories: 500   Protein: 44.0 g
Carbohydrate: 11.1 g Fat: 30.6 g

* The famous Digby scallops are bay scallops, the sweetest and most succulent of the scallop species. Bay scallops average 100 per pound (500 g) while sea scallops average 30 per pound (500 g). Digby, Nova Scotia is home to the largest inshore scallop fleet in the world.

garlic, shrimp & jarlsberg frittata

An elegant frittata for two, make it whenever you have something to celebrate. You can also substitute smoked Gouda for smoked Jarlsberg. It's still fabulous!

2 eggs	2
1½ tbsp light cream	22 mL
1½ tsp finely chopped fresh chives	7 mL
1½ tbsp butter	22 mL
½ tsp minced fresh garlic	2 mL
12 raw shrimp, shelled, deveined	12
1 cup finely grated smoked Jarlsberg cheese*	250 mL

Makes 2 servings
Preparation: 8 minutes
Cooking: 8 minutes

Nutrients per serving
Calories: 402　　　Protein: 26.7 g
Carbohydrate: 2.9 g　　Fat: 31.3 g

1　Whisk eggs, cream and chives until light and frothy. Set aside.

2　Melt butter in a medium non-stick skillet over medium-high heat. As soon as butter melts, add garlic; cook until golden. Add shrimp; cook for 1 minute per side, or until pink.

3　Turn heat to medium; pour egg mixture evenly over shrimp. As mixture sets at the edges, with spatula, gently lift cooked portion to allow uncooked egg to flow underneath. Cook until bottom is set and top is almost set.

4　Sprinkle cheese evenly over frittata. Cover skillet and turn off the heat. Let stand until cheese is melted.

5　Cut the frittata into wedges and serve immediately.

Louise MacDonald
Middle Sackville, Nova Scotia

* Jarlsberg, like Swiss cheese, has irregular holes throughout. Originating from Norway, Jarlsberg has a mild, slightly sweet flavour similar to Swiss cheese. It is suitable for cooking and for slicing as an appetizer.

spicy goat cheese & shrimp omelette

This fabulous flavour combination is perfect for a special dinner. Quick and easy, this omelette could be served on many occasions, from an alfresco summer evening to an after-the-theatre supper.

4 eggs	4	
4 tbsp water	60 mL	
fines herbes*, salt and pepper to taste		
1 tsp olive oil	5 mL	
4 tbsp salsa	60 mL	
3½ oz cooked medium or large shrimp, shelled, deveined	100 g	
2 oz goat cheese**	60 g	

Makes 2 to 3 servings
Preparation: 6 minutes
Cooking: 10 minutes

1 Whisk eggs, water and seasonings together in a medium bowl.

2 Heat oil in a medium non-stick skillet over medium heat.

3 Pour egg mixture into skillet. As mixture sets at the edges, with spatula, gently lift cooked portion to allow uncooked egg to flow underneath. Cook until bottom is set and top is almost set.

4 Top half of the omelette with salsa, shrimp and cheese. Fold other half over filling.

5 Serve on a warm plate.

Nutrients per serving
Calories: 199   Protein: 18.9 g
Carbohydrate: 1.9 g   Fat: 12.5 g

Denise Loiselle
Montreal, Quebec

* Fines herbes (fi:nz'erb) is a finely chopped blend of herbs, usually chives, chervil, tarragon and parsley, and sometimes including marjoram, savory and watercress. It is available commercially in bottled form.

** Goat cheese (chèvre) has a wonderful fresh sharp/tart flavour. The texture may range from creamy to semi-firm. Chèvre is originally from France, but several Canadian cheese makers are now making excellent chèvres. *Pur chèvre* indicates that only goat's milk was used in making the cheese.

shrimp delight omelette

A combination of cooked seafood could be substituted for the shrimp to make a cornucopia of flavours. This very attractive, tasty omelette could easily be doubled or tripled.

2 tbsp butter	30 mL	
2 tbsp sliced green onion	30 mL	
4 tsp all-purpose flour	20 mL	
dried basil to taste		
salt and pepper to taste		
½ cup milk	125 mL	
½ cup cooked shrimp	125 mL	
2 tbsp low-fat sour cream	30 mL	
4 eggs	4	
1 tbsp water	15 mL	

1 Melt butter in a small saucepan over low heat. When butter begins to brown, add green onion. Cook until onion is tender, about 2 minutes.

2 Sprinkle flour, basil, salt and pepper over onion. Slowly stir in milk. Cook and stir until mixture bubbles and thickens.

3 Stir in shrimp; heat through.

4 Remove the pan from the heat. Stir in sour cream. Keep warm.

5 Whisk eggs, water, salt and pepper together in a small bowl.

6 Spray a small non-stick skillet with cooking spray. Preheat to medium.

7 Pour half of egg mixture into skillet. As mixture sets at the edges, with spatula, gently lift cooked portion to allow uncooked egg to flow underneath. Cook until bottom is set and top is almost set.

8 Spoon half of the filling along the centre of the omelette. Fold both sides of omelette over filling and transfer to a warm plate.

9 Repeat the process to make a second omelette.

Makes 2 servings
Preparation: 7 minutes
Cooking: 20 minutes

Nutrients per serving
Calories: 347   Protein: 22.8 g
Carbohydrate: 9.6 g   Fat: 23.7 g

Sandra Cohen
Mississauga, Ontario

lobster omelette

You'll be tempted to make two omelettes for a romantic dinner or brunch. For a fabulous variation, add a drizzle of melted butter and a squeeze of lemon juice to the filling.

½ cup chopped, cooked lobster	125 mL	
¼ cup chopped celery	50 mL	
2 tbsp chopped fresh chives	30 mL	
2 tbsp chopped green onion	30 mL	
2 eggs	2	
2 tbsp water	30 mL	
salt and pepper to taste		

Makes 1 serving
Preparation: 15 minutes
Cooking: 4 minutes

1 Combine lobster, celery, chives and green onion in a small bowl; set aside.

2 Whisk eggs, water, salt and pepper together in another bowl.

3 Spray a small non-stick skillet with cooking spray. Preheat to medium.

4 Pour egg mixture into skillet. As mixture sets at the edges, with spatula, gently lift cooked portion to allow uncooked egg to flow underneath. Cook until bottom is set and top is almost set.

5 Spoon lobster filling over half of the omelette. Fold other half over filling.

6 Serve on a warm plate.

Nutrients per serving
Calories: 227 Protein: 27.8 g
Carbohydrate: 3.8 g Fat: 10.4 g

Mavis Burton
Corner Brook, Newfoundland

gaspé salmon *frittata*

Easy and delicious — broil the salmon or cook it quickly in the microwave.

3 tbsp vegetable oil	45 mL
3 tbsp EACH chopped onion, green pepper and celery	45 mL
4 eggs	4
½ cup milk	125 mL
¼ tsp salt	1 mL
freshly ground pepper to taste	
½ tsp wheat germ (optional)	2 mL
¼ tsp salted herbs*	1 mL
1 cup flaked cooked salmon OR 7.5 oz (225 g) can salmon, drained, flaked	250 mL

1. Preheat oven to 350°F (180°C).
2. Heat oil in a medium ovenproof skillet over medium heat. Turn heat to low.
3. Sauté onion, peppers and celery until lightly golden, about 3 minutes.
4. Whisk eggs, milk, salt, pepper, wheat germ and herbs in a medium bowl.
5. Pour eggs into skillet. Sprinkle salmon over frittata.
6. Bake in preheated oven for 20 to 30 minutes, or until eggs are set and frittata is puffy.
7. Serve with baked potatoes, a salad or green vegetables.

Makes 4 servings
Preparation: 10 minutes
Cooking: 30 minutes

Diane Charette
St-Étienne-des-Grès, Quebec

Nutrients per serving
Calories: 244   Protein: 16.0 g
Carbohydrate: 3.1 g   Fat: 18.4 g

* Also available in a commercial mixture, salted herbs (herbes salées) are a Quebec and Acadian specialty. They are a combination of chives, savoury, parsley, chervil, celery leaves, green onions and grated carrots preserved in coarse salt. If you can't find them, use a blend of the herbs you most like to serve with salmon such as dill, thyme, parsley, garlic and/or chives. Add a pinch of salt for good measure.

brie & smoked salmon omelette

Luxurious flavours and silky texture – brie and smoked salmon melt into this marvellous omelette.

2 eggs	2
1 tbsp soy milk*	15 mL
¼ cup chopped green pepper	50 mL
2 tbsp chopped onion	30 mL
salt and pepper to taste	
1 oz Brie cheese	30 g
1 oz smoked salmon	30 g

Makes 1 generous serving
Preparation: 5 minutes
Cooking: 4 minutes

Nutrients per serving
Calories: 295   Protein: 24.3 g
Carbohydrate: 5.1 g   Fat: 19.3 g

1 Whisk eggs and soy milk together in a small bowl.

2 Spray a small non-stick skillet with cooking spray. Heat skillet over medium heat.

3 Sauté green peppers and onion over medium heat until soft, about 4 minutes.

4 Pour eggs into skillet over vegetables. Sprinkle lightly with salt and pepper. As eggs set at the edges, with spatula, gently lift cooked portion to allow uncooked egg to flow underneath. Cook until eggs are almost set, 3 to 4 minutes.

5 Arrange slices of Brie and smoked salmon on half of the omelette. Fold other half over filling.

6 Slide the omelette onto a warm plate.

Lianne Landry
Dartmouth, Nova Scotia

* Soybean milk is rich in iron and contains more protein than cow's milk. It is cholesterol-free, low in fat and sodium, and is a very good milk substitute for people with milk allergies. Made by pressing ground cooked soybeans, soy milk is curdled to make tofu. Adding acids such as vinegar, lemon juice or wine will curdle soy milk.

mushroom & tuna frittata

This frittata has a nice flavour balance. The tuna is there, but doesn't overwhelm.
This dish is also tasty without cheese.

6 eggs	6	1	Whisk eggs with salt and pepper in a medium bowl until frothy. Stir in tuna; mix well. Stir in mushrooms and green peppers.
salt and pepper to taste			
3.3 oz* flaked light tuna, drained, mashed	93 g		
3 medium mushrooms, sliced	3	2	Spray a medium non-stick skillet with cooking spray. Preheat to medium.
1 small green pepper, chopped	1	3	Pour egg mixture into skillet. As mixture sets at the edges, with spatula, gently lift cooked portion to allow uncooked egg to flow underneath. Cook until bottom is set and top is almost set.
1/3 cup shredded marble cheese	75 mL		

4 Slide the omelette onto a plate. Place skillet over plate. Flip frittata back into skillet. Cook 2 more minutes.**

Makes 3 servings
Preparation: 7 minutes
Cooking: 10 minutes

5 Transfer frittata to plate. Sprinkle with cheese, salt and pepper.

Nutrients per serving
Calories: 233   Protein: 21.7 g
Carbohydrate: 3.3 g   Fat: 14.3 g

Bonnie Cuthbertson
Simcoe, Ontario

* This amount is half of a 6.5 oz (185 g) can.

** If you prefer, use an ovenproof skillet and place under a preheated broiler for a few seconds to set frittata top.

chicken & ginger omelette

Plan to make this often when you have leftover cooked chicken.
The combination of chicken, ginger and honey is outstanding!

⅓ cup minced cooked chicken	75 mL	
1 green onion, minced	1	
1 tbsp minced fresh ginger	15 mL	
2 tsp honey	10 mL	
1 tsp sesame seeds	5 mL	
salt and pepper to taste		
2 eggs	2	
2 tbsp chicken broth	30 mL	

1 Combine chicken, onion, ginger, honey and sesame seeds in a small bowl. Sprinkle with salt and pepper. Set aside.

2 Whisk eggs with chicken broth in a small bowl.

3 Spray a medium non-stick skillet with cooking spray. Preheat to medium.

4 Pour egg mixture into skillet. As mixture sets at the edges, with spatula, lift cooked portion to allow uncooked egg to flow underneath. Cook until eggs are set, about 4 minutes.

5 Spoon chicken mixture over half of the omelette. Fold other half over filling.

6 Serve on a warm plate.

Makes 1 serving
Preparation: 5 minutes
Cooking: 5 minutes

Nutrients per serving
Calories: 312   Protein: 27.8 g
Carbohydrate: 15.3 g Fat: 15.3 g

Claudette Gauthier
Trois-Rivières, Quebec

spicy chicken omelette

This is a delicious presentation for leftover barbecued chicken. A delicate omelette, with a higher than usual proportion of milk, it may be a bit difficult to fold. You could set the skillet under the broiler for a minute, to set the top, and serve it in wedges like a frittata.

3 eggs	3	1
½ cup milk	125 mL	
1 barbecued chicken breast, diced	1	2
¼ cup chopped green onion	50 mL	3
¼ cup chopped red onion	50 mL	4
minced hot banana peppers to taste		
cayenne pepper to taste		
¼ cup shredded cheese	50 mL	5

1 Whisk eggs and milk together in a small bowl.

2 Spray a medium non-stick skillet with cooking spray. Preheat to medium.

3 Pour egg mixture into skillet.

4 Add chicken, onions and banana peppers to skillet. As eggs set at the edges, with spatula, gently lift cooked portion to allow uncooked egg to flow underneath. Cook until almost set, about 8 minutes.

5 Sprinkle cayenne and cheese on half of the omelette. Fold other half over cheese.

6 Cut omelette in half and serve with nacho chips and sour cream.

Makes 2 servings
Preparation: 14 minutes
Cooking: 10 minutes

Nutrients per serving
Calories: 290   Protein: 29.0 g
Carbohydrate: 6.2 g   Fat: 16.0 g

Sherrie Guthrie
Ottawa, Ontario

simple summer omelette

Fresh dill is delectable with eggs. It is also a great flavour accent for broccoli and zucchini.

2 eggs	2	
2 tbsp milk	30 mL	
1 tbsp minced fresh dill	15 mL	
2 tbsp diced ham OR smoked turkey	30 mL	
salt and pepper to taste		
¼ cup chopped broccoli	50 mL	
¼ cup thinly sliced zucchini	50 mL	
2 tbsp shredded Monterey Jack cheese	30 mL	
fruit chutney* for garnish		

Makes 1 serving
Preparation: 10 minutes
Cooking: 8 minutes

1 Beat eggs and milk together in a small bowl. Stir in dill, ham or turkey, salt and pepper. Set aside.

2 Spray a small non-stick skillet with cooking spray. Preheat to medium.

3 Sauté broccoli and zucchini until just tender, about 2 minutes.

4 Pour egg mixture into skillet with sautéed vegetables. Cook until eggs are almost set, lifting edges of omelette during cooking to allow uncooked egg to flow underneath.

5 Sprinkle cheese on half of the omelette. Fold other half over cheese.

6 Serve with your favourite fruit chutney.

Nutrients per serving
Calories: 251   Protein: 22.0 g
Carbohydrate: 4.6 g   Fat: 15.8 g

Jan Taylor
London, Ontario

* Spicy fruit chutneys, flavoured with ginger, were developed in India as condiments to accompany curry dishes. The range of chutneys has expanded from the traditional mango to include peach, apple, pear, green tomato, etc. Chutney may be smooth or chunky in texture and the flavours range from sweet to hot.

ham, cheese & vegetable omelette

This is an opportunity to turn last night's leftover vegetables into a quick and tasty meal.
Substitute Swiss or your favourite cheese for the Cheddar, if you wish.

2 eggs	2
salt and pepper to taste	
1 green onion, chopped	1
1 slice ham, chopped	1 slice
2 tbsp chopped green pepper	30 mL
2 tbsp EACH cooked green peas and corn	30 mL
2 tbsp shredded Cheddar cheese	30 mL

Makes 1 serving
Preparation: 7 minutes
Cooking: 7 minutes

1   Whisk eggs, salt and pepper together in a small bowl.

2   Spray a medium non-stick skillet with cooking spray.

3   Sauté green onion, ham and green peppers over medium heat for 2 to 3 minutes, or until vegetables are soft. Remove from skillet and keep warm. If peas and corn are cold, add them to the skillet for the final minute of cooking.

4   Pour eggs into the same skillet. Cook over medium heat until eggs are set, about 4 minutes. As eggs set at the edges, with spatula, gently lift cooked portion to allow uncooked egg to flow underneath.

5   Spoon ham mixture over half of the omelette, along with peas, corn and cheese. Fold other half over filling.

Nutrients per serving
Calories: 281   Protein: 23.4 g
Carbohydrate: 10.2 g   Fat: 16.2 g

William Coughlin
Tyne Valley, Prince Edward Island

a dilly of an omelette

Dilly-icious! Serve with toasted English muffins and garnish with fresh strawberries.

4 eggs	4	
1 tbsp milk	15 mL	
2 tsp chopped fresh dill	10 mL	
2 tsp chopped chives	10 mL	
salt and pepper to taste		
½ cup shredded Havarti Dill cheese	125 mL	
½ cup diced Black Forest ham	125 mL	

1. Whisk eggs, milk, dill, chives, salt and pepper together in a medium bowl.
2. Spray a medium non-stick skillet with cooking spray. Preheat to medium.
3. Pour eggs into skillet. As eggs set at the edges, with spatula, gently lift cooked portion to allow uncooked egg to flow underneath. Cook until bottom is set and top is almost set.
4. Add cheese and ham to half of the omelette. Fold other half over filling.

Makes 2 servings
Preparation: 8 minutes
Cooking: 6 minutes

Nutrients per serving
Calories: 317   Protein: 27.5 g
Carbohydrate: 1.7 g   Fat: 22.3 g

Judy Graschuk
Edmonton, Alberta

reuben omelette

Try this with or without sauerkraut – it's mouthwatering.

4-6 slices deli corned beef	4-6	
1 tsp butter OR oil	5 mL	
6 eggs	6	
1 tbsp water	15 mL	
1 cup sauerkraut, drained	250 mL	
½ cup shredded Swiss cheese	125 mL	

1. Dice corned beef. Sauté in butter in a large non-stick skillet over medium heat for 2 minutes.
2. Whisk eggs with water. Pour into skillet over corned beef. As mixture sets at the edges, lift cooked portion to allow uncooked egg to flow underneath.
3. Spoon sauerkraut over half of the omelette. Cover with cheese. Turn off heat. Cover skillet for 2 minutes to warm sauerkraut and melt cheese.
4. Fold omelette over filling; cut into 3 portions. Serve with rye toast.

Makes 3 servings
Preparation: 6 minutes
Cooking: 12 minutes

Nutrients per serving
Calories: 310   Protein: 25.5 g
Carbohydrate: 5.0 g   Fat: 20.4 g

Stacey Wellbrock
Calgary, Alberta

bacon omelette

This satisfying omelette has a light fluffy texture and mellow flavour.
It tastes terrific with chunky homemade tomato salsa.

½ cup diced bacon, about 3 slices	125 mL	
1 cup mashed potatoes	250 mL	
2 tbsp milk	30 mL	
1 tsp baking powder	5 mL	
½ tsp salt	2 mL	
pepper to taste		
4 egg yolks, beaten		4
4 egg whites, whipped until stiff		4
grated cheese (optional)		

Makes 2 to 4 servings
Preparation: 8 minutes
Cooking: 20 minutes

1 Cook bacon until crisp in a large non-stick skillet, about 6 minutes. Transfer bacon to a small dish. Pour off drippings.

2 Stir mashed potatoes, milk, baking powder, salt, pepper and egg yolks together in a medium bowl.

3 Fold stiffly beaten egg whites into mashed potato mixture.

4 Spray same skillet with cooking spray. Preheat until hot.

5 Pour egg mixture into skillet. Smooth top.

6 Sprinkle bacon over omelette. Cover skillet and cook over low heat until puffed and brown on the bottom, about 10 minutes.

7 Fold omelette and top with cheese, if desired. Cut into wedges and serve.

Chico Dedick
Delta, British Columbia

Nutrients per serving
Calories: 180   Protein: 10.4 g
Carbohydrate: 11.6 g Fat: 10.1 g

swiss, bacon 'n' mushroom frittata

This is perfect for a light dinner. Serve with sliced tomatoes and a green salad.

3 cups sliced mushrooms	750 mL	
1/3 cup sliced green onion	75 mL	
1 tbsp flour	15 mL	
1/2 tsp salt	2 mL	
6 eggs	6	
3/4 cup milk	175 mL	
2 cups shredded Swiss, Havarti OR Cheddar cheese	500 mL	
1 tbsp grated Parmesan cheese	15 mL	
8 slices bacon, cooked, crumbled	8 slices	

1 Sauté mushrooms and onion in a medium non-stick skillet until all liquid has evaporated. Sprinkle flour and salt over vegetables; toss to coat.

2 Whisk eggs and milk together in a large bowl. Stir in mushroom mixture and 1 1/2 cups (375 mL) cheese.

3 Pour egg mixture into the same skillet. Turn heat to low; cover and cook for 15 to 25 minutes, or until set.

4 Sprinkle Parmesan, remaining Swiss cheese and bacon over frittata. If skillet is ovenproof, place under broiler until cheese melts, or cover skillet until cheese melts.

Makes 4 to 6 servings
Preparation: 10 minutes
Cooking: 15 minutes

Jane Covey
Beaver Bank, Nova Scotia

Nutrients per serving
Calories: 309   Protein: 21.9 g
Carbohydrate: 5.8 g   Fat: 21.9 g

stampede dinner omelette

Hearty and satisfying, serve to three hungry cowboys with a side of salsa, fresh carrot sticks and a green salad.

1 tbsp oil	15 mL	
¼ cup chopped onion	50 mL	
8 oz extra-lean ground beef	250 g	
2 tsp taco seasoning	10 mL	
6 eggs	6	
4 tbsp water	60 mL	
2 tbsp canned green chilies, OR 1 tsp (5 mL) chopped jalapeño pepper	30 mL	
1 medium tomato, chopped	1	
¼ cup finely crushed taco chips	50 mL	
¼ cup shredded Monterey Jack cheese	50 mL	

1 Heat oil in a large non-stick skillet over medium-high heat. Add onion; sauté for 1 minute.

2 Crumble ground beef into skillet over onion. Add taco seasoning. Sauté until well done. Drain and set aside.

3 Whisk eggs with water in a small bowl.

4 Heat the same skillet over medium-high heat.

5 Pour eggs into skillet. As eggs set at the edges, with spatula, gently lift cooked portion to allow uncooked egg to flow underneath. Cook until bottom is set and top is almost set.

6 Spoon beef mixture over half of the omelette. Layer chilies, tomato, taco chips and cheese over beef.

7 Fold other half of omelette over the layered filling.

8 Turn heat to low. Cover skillet and cook until the filling is hot and cheese is melted.

Makes 3 generous servings
Preparation: 13 minutes
Cooking: 17 minutes

Charlene Schmitt
Calgary, Alberta

Nutrients per serving
Calories: 438   Protein: 34.0 g
Carbohydrate: 10.1 g   Fat: 28.4 g

genoa salami *frittata*

Leftovers taste great heated and tucked between slices of toasted multi-grain bread.

12 eggs	12	1	Whisk eggs with milk in a small bowl.
1 tbsp milk	15 mL	2	Stir-fry salami over medium heat in a large non-stick skillet for 4 minutes.
¼ lb Genoa salami, thinly sliced	125 g	3	Pour eggs into skillet. As eggs set at the edges, with spatula, gently lift cooked portion to allow uncooked egg to flow underneath. Cook until bottom is set and top is almost set.

Makes 5 servings
Preparation: 4 minutes
Cooking: 14 minutes

4   Cut into wedges to serve.

Nutrients per serving
Calories: 234   Protein: 18.0 g
Carbohydrate: 1.9 g   Fat: 16.5 g

Wendy Marion
Regina, Saskatchewan

asian pork *omelette*

Serve with rice and creative toppings – chutney, salsa, soy sauce or plum sauce.

6 oz lean ground pork	175 g	1	Crumble pork into a preheated medium non-stick skillet. Add onion; cook on medium-high until pork is no longer pink. Set aside.
1 medium onion, chopped	1		
6 eggs	6		
¼ cup water	50 mL	2	Whisk eggs with water, fish sauce and seasonings in a small bowl.
½ tsp fish sauce or to taste	2 mL	3	Wipe skillet and spray with cooking spray. Preheat to medium.
salt and pepper to taste			

4   Pour eggs into skillet. Cook until set, lifting omelette edges to allow uncooked egg to flow underneath.

Makes 3 to 4 servings
Preparation: 5 minutes
Cooking: 18 minutes

5   Spoon pork mixture over half of the omelette. Fold omelette over filling.

Nutrients per serving
Calories: 190   Protein: 17.2 g
Carbohydrate: 2.8 g   Fat: 11.7 g

Dennis Lowe
Regina, Saskatchewan

fuzzy navel omelette,
page 116

desserts

fuzzy navel omelette

This beautiful fruit-filled omelette lends itself to variations. Try mangoes or nectarines, use mint instead of parsley and add minced crystallized ginger to the filling or for a garnish.

2 tbsp butter	30 mL
2 peaches, peeled, sliced	2
2 tbsp peach schnapps	30 mL
4 eggs	4
1 tbsp water	15 mL
1 tbsp chopped parsley	15 mL
¼ cup grated cheese, Cheddar OR Emmenthal (optional)	50 mL
whipped cream for garnish	

Makes 2 servings
Preparation: 7½ minutes
Cooking: 14 minutes

Nutrients per serving
Calories: 307   Protein: 13.0 g
Carbohydrate: 8.9 g   Fat: 21.5 g

1 Melt butter in a small saucepan over low heat. Add peaches; cook until warm. Remove pan from stove. Stir in schnapps. Set aside and keep warm.

2 Beat eggs with water and parsley.

3 Spray a small non-stick skillet with cooking spray. Preheat to medium.

4 Pour half of the egg mixture into the skillet. As mixture sets at the edges, with spatula, gently lift cooked portion to allow uncooked egg to flow underneath. Cook until bottom is set and top is almost set.

5 Spoon half of the peach filling along centre of the omelette. Sprinkle with half of the cheese. Fold both sides of omelette over filling.

6 Transfer omelette to a warm plate. Repeat for the second omelette.

7 Drizzle any leftover filling liquid over omelettes and garnish with whipped cream and peach slices.

Sandra Cohen
Mississauga, Ontario

fresh fruit & yogurt omelette*

Sliced nectarines or peaches, fresh blueberries and low-fat vanilla yogurt are a delicious, light-tasting combination. This makes a lovely dessert or breakfast treat.

3 eggs	**3**
salt to taste	
1½ cups sliced fruit OR **berries** OR **a combination of both**	**375 mL**
½ cup low-fat yogurt OR **low-fat whipped cream**	**125 mL**
2 tbsp maple syrup	**30 mL**

Makes 2 servings
Preparation: 5 minutes
Cooking: 8 minutes

1 Whisk eggs with salt in a small bowl.

2 Spray a medium non-stick skillet with cooking spray. Preheat to medium-hot.

3 Pour eggs into skillet. As eggs set at the edges, with spatula, gently lift cooked portion to allow uncooked egg to flow underneath. Cook until bottom is set and top is almost set.

4 Top half of the omelette with fruit. Fold other half over fruit. Cook for 1 more minute.

5 Cut the omelette in half. Place each half on a warm plate. Garnish with yogurt or low-fat whipped cream.

6 Drizzle with maple syrup.

Nutrients per serving
Calories: 259   Protein: 13.4 g
Carbohydrate: 32.7 g Fat: 8.9 g

Kim Dukart
Calgary, Alberta

* This is a heart-healthy omelette.

fruit omelette with maple sugar*

Lovely, light and adaptable – use your favourite fruit combination. If you don't have maple sugar, use brown sugar. Also, try topping this omelette with a dollop of sweetened light sour cream or low-fat vanilla yogurt.

2 eggs	2	1	Whisk eggs in a small bowl.
½ banana, sliced	½	2	Spray a small non-stick skillet with cooking spray. Preheat to medium.
4-6 fresh strawberries, sliced	4-6	3	Pour eggs into skillet. As eggs set at the edges, with spatula, gently lift cooked portion to allow uncooked egg to flow underneath. Cook until bottom is set and top is almost set.
½ apple, peeled or unpeeled, thinly sliced	½		
1 tsp maple sugar**, or more, to taste	5 mL	4	Arrange fruit on half of the omelette. Sprinkle generously with maple sugar. Fold the omelette over fruit.

Makes 1 serving
Preparation: 5 minutes
Cooking: 4 minutes

5 Serve on a warm plate.

Nutrients per serving
Calories: 283   Protein: 13.4 g
Carbohydrate: 35.6 g   Fat: 10.6 g

Sophie Daviau
Ste-Cécile-de-Milton, Quebec

** Maple sugar is twice as sweet as white sugar. It is made by boiling sugar maple sap until the liquid has almost evaporated.

* This is a heart-healthy omelette.

cream cheese & pineapple omelette

Luscious flavours sparked with ginger – this is a favourite.

2 eggs	2	
2 tbsp water	30 mL	
1 tbsp cream cheese	15 mL	
¼ cup crushed pineapple, drained	50 mL	
ground ginger OR minced crystallized ginger to taste		

Makes 1 serving
Preparation: 3 minutes
Cooking: 4 minutes

1 Whisk eggs and water together.

2 Spray a non-stick skillet with cooking spray. Preheat to medium.

3 Pour eggs into skillet. As eggs set at the edges, with spatula, gently lift cooked portion to allow uncooked egg to flow underneath. Cook until bottom is set and top is almost set.

4 Add cream cheese, pineapple and ginger to half of omelette. Fold and serve.

Nutrients per serving
Calories: 233   Protein: 13.7 g
Carbohydrate: 10.7 g   Fat: 15.0 g

Jean MacArthur
Moncton, New Brunswick

sugar baby omelette

This omelette could also be filled with fruit and rolled or folded. Try it with pecans.

2 eggs	2	
2 tsp brown sugar	10 mL	
⅓ cup chopped, toasted almonds	75 mL	
salt to taste		
½ tsp butter	2 mL	

Makes 1 serving
Preparation: 7 minutes
Cooking: 5 minutes

1 Whisk eggs until well blended. Stir in brown sugar, almonds and salt.

2 Melt butter in a small non-stick skillet. Preheat to medium-hot.

3 Pour egg mixture into skillet. Cook until mixture is set, lifting cooked portion to allow uncooked egg to flow underneath.

4 Serve with sliced bananas or peaches or your favourite fruit.

Nutrients per serving
Calories: 473   Protein: 23.4 g
Carbohydrate: 19.5 g   Fat: 35.5 g

Bamini Jayabalasingham
Toronto, Ontario

grandma's blintzes*

This very tasty omelette is even better with a layer of thinly sliced, sweetened strawberries or peaches tucked into the omelette with the cottage cheese.

1 egg	**1**
2 tbsp cottage cheese	**30 mL**
cinnamon to taste	
sugar OR sweetener to taste	

1 Whisk egg in a small bowl.

2 Spray a small non-stick skillet with cooking spray. Preheat to medium.

3 Pour egg into skillet. As egg sets at the edges, with spatula, gently lift cooked portion to allow uncooked egg to flow underneath. Cook until bottom is set and top is almost set.

4 Flip the omelette over and cook the second side for 1 minute.

5 Slide the omelette onto a warm plate. Spoon cottage cheese over the omelette. Roll up.

6 Sprinkle top of omelette with cinnamon and sugar.

Makes 1 serving
Preparation: 2 minutes
Cooking: 5 minutes

Nutrients per serving
Calories: 98   Protein: 10.0 g
Carbohydrate: 1.3 g   Fat: 5.5 g

Avril Bell
Sherwood Park, Alberta

* This is a heart-healthy omelette.

note

Traditionally, a blintz is a crêpe or very thin pancake. It is rolled around either sweet or savoury fillings.

warm memories

This fragrant omelette makes a delicious dessert. Accompanied by a fresh fruit salad and warm muffins, it is also perfect for brunch. Try sprinkling a bit of brown sugar on the Brie before you fold the omelette.

4 eggs	**4**	
cinnamon to taste		
4 slices, Brie cheese (about 2 oz/60g)	**4 slices**	
2 tbsp raisins	**30 mL**	
2 tbsp chopped walnuts	**30 mL**	

1. Whisk eggs with cinnamon in a small bowl.

2. Spray a medium non-stick skillet with cooking spray. Preheat to medium.

3. Pour eggs into skillet. As eggs set at the edges, with spatula, gently lift cooked portion to allow uncooked egg to flow underneath. Cook until eggs are almost set, about 5 minutes.

4. Place Brie, raisins and walnuts on half of the omelette. Fold other half over filling. Let stand for 2 minutes to melt the Brie.

5. Cut the omelette in half. Place each half on a warm plate.

Makes 2 servings
Preparation: 3 minutes
Cooking: 7 minutes

Nutrients per serving
Calories: 319   Protein: 19.6 g
Carbohydrate: 9.4 g   Fat: 22.9 g

Justin Hodkinson
Victoria, British Columbia

magic rainbow omelette*

This one is for the young and the young at heart. This whimsical omelette with a fun look might be just the thing to get finicky little eaters to sample eggs and benefit from their excellent nutritional value.

2 eggs	**2**	
1 tsp colourful sprinkles * *	**5 mL**	
⅓ cup shredded Cheddar cheese (optional)	**75 mL**	

Makes 1 serving
Preparation: 2 minutes
Cooking: 4 minutes

Nutrients per serving (excluding cheese)
Calories: 159   Protein: 12.3 g
Carbohydrate: 4.2 g   Fat: 9.9 g

1 Whisk eggs in a small bowl.

2 Spray a small non-stick skillet with cooking spray. Preheat to medium.

3 Pour eggs into skillet. Cook until eggs are set, then flip and cook the second side.

4 Add sprinkles while second side cooks. If desired, also add cheese when omelette is flipped. Fold and add more sprinkles.

5 Slide onto a serving plate.

Angela Seury
Quesnel, British Columbia

* This is a heart-healthy omelette.

* * Sprinkles or décors, used for decorating cookies and cupcakes, range from brilliant colourful sugar crystals to tiny multicoloured candy balls and sparkling sanding sugars.

Rod-shaped chocolate or multi-coloured candy sprinkles are also called "jimmies".

omelettes index

omelettes index

share omelettes – perfect anytime with a friend

Omelettes – Perfect Anytime _____ x $15.95 = $ _____

shipping and handling charge (total order) _____ = $ 4.00

subtotal _____ = $ _____

in Canada add 7% GST _____ = $ _____

total enclosed _____ = $ _____

U.S. and international orders payable in U.S. funds/prices subject to change.

name: _____

street: _____

city: _____ prov./state: _____

country: _____ postal code/zip: _____

telephone (in case we have a question about your order): _____

❐ cheque OR charge to ❐ visa ❐ mastercard

account number: | | | | | | | | | | | | | | | | |

expiry date: | | | |

signature: _____

make cheque or money order payable to:

Centax Books & Distribution
1150 Eighth Avenue
Regina, Saskatchewan
Canada   S4R 1C9

OR

order by phone, fax or email:
phone: 1-800-667-5595
fax: 1-800-823-6829
e-mail: centax@printwest.com

See our Web site for the complete range of Centax cookbooks, gardening books, history books, etc.
www.centaxbooks.com

For fund-raising or volume purchases, contact Centax Books & Distribution for volume rates. Please allow 2 to 3 weeks for delivery.

omelettes **perfect anytime**